8-18-01

Joanne -

Here's to
your continued
good health.

Love,
Carrie

The Healing Garden

GAYLE POVIS ALLEMAN, M.S., R.D.

CONSULTANTS: SILENA HERON, N.D. AND ERIC YARNELL, N.D.

ILLUSTRATIONS: JACQUI MORGAN

PUBLICATIONS INTERNATIONAL, LTD.

Contributing Writer:
Gayle Povis Alleman, M.S., R.D., holds degrees in both alternative and conventional nutrition. She manages the nutrition education program for Washington State University Cooperative Extension and teaches nutrition at Bastyr University and other colleges. She is also a freelance writer and speaker in the area of food, nutrition, and health, specializing in holistic nutrition to promote optimum health.

Consultants:
Dr. Silena Heron is a naturopathic physician with a family health care practice. She is a nationally recognized specialist in botanical medicine who has taught throughout the West and Canada since 1973. She was founding chair of botanical medicine at Bastyr University and was on its faculty for six years. Currently, she is an adjunct faculty member at Southwest College of Naturopathic Medicine. Dr. Heron is technical consultant to a botanical pharmaceutical company. She is also the founding vice president of the Botanical Medicine Academy, an accrediting organization for the clinical use of herbal medicines.

Dr. Eric Yarnell is a naturopathic physician, author, editor, and lecturer. He serves as research editor for the *Journal of Naturopathic Medicine* and teaches at the Southwest College of Naturopathic Medicine. He is co-author of *The Phytotherapy Research Compendium* and a contributor to *The Natural Pharmacy*. Dr. Yarnell helped found and is currently treasurer of the Botanical Medicine Academy.

Other contributing writers: Densie Webb, Ph.D., R.D.; Susan Male Smith, M.A., R.D.; Jill Stansbury, N.D.

Note: Neither Publications International, Ltd., nor the authors, consultants, editors, or publisher take responsibility for any possible consequences from any treatment, procedure, exercise, dietary modification, action, or application of medication or preparation by any person reading or following the information in this book. The publication of this book does not constitute the practice of medicine, and this book does not attempt to replace your physician or your pharmacist. Before undertaking any course of treatment, the authors, consultants, editors, and publisher advise the reader to check with a physician or other health care provider.

CONTENTS

ILLNESSES AND THEIR GARDEN HEALERS • 194

INDEX • 247

GROWING A HEALING GARDEN is therapeutic and satisfying in many different ways. It is an activity that nurtures the body, the mind, and the spirit. Working the soil—lifting, digging, carrying, bending, raking—is an excellent form of exercise, strengthening and toning muscles that might otherwise be idle. And the garden draws you out into the fresh air and sunshine, allowing the sun's energy to trigger brain chemicals that promote a feeling of well-being.

Many gardeners find that gardening is a form of meditation. Alone with your thoughts and with nature, it is easy to relax. Your mind may wander while your hands tend your fledgling plants. You may feel acutely aware of the interconnectedness of all living things, sensing Mother Nature's rhythm and your place in it. Gardening will give you a new appreciation of and respect for the beauty and order of the natural world.

The fruits (and vegetables and herbs!) of your labor in the garden yield edible rewards, too. The products of your garden are the tangible link between the spiritual and the physical benefits of gardening. Foods and herbs are loaded with health-promoting constituents, including phytochemicals, vitamins, and minerals. Phytochemicals can kill bacteria and viruses, mimic estrogen, enhance immune function, and ward off cancer and other diseases. Vitamins and minerals help us maintain normal metabolism and the structure of living tissues, and they regulate important body processes. Plant foods also contain a group of vitamins, minerals, and enzymes called antioxidants that help prevent cell damage and, ultimately, diseases such as cancer, heart disease, cataracts, and arthritis. Growing and eating a variety of foods, then, helps reduce your risk of developing life-threatening diseases as well as less serious infections and conditions.

The healing garden provides other benefits, too. Growing your own produce, herbs, and flowers is economical. Herbs cost next to nothing when harvested from the garden. And having a selection of fresh herbs on hand may open your mind and palate to new flavors. Flowers from your garden are likely to bring greater joy than expensive, short-lived flowers from the florist. And fresh fruits and vegetables—well, they certainly are less expensive than those from the grocery store or farmer's market. Vegetables and fruits picked fresh from your garden taste so delicious, you'll wonder how you settled for store-bought produce. You'll probably eat more of them, just because they're so good, and as a result you will be even healthier and more resistant to illness.

This book is a guide to growing a healing garden, one that is tailor-made to your geograph-ical area and your own particular health requirements. The first section explains how to plan your garden and how to prepare it for optimal growing conditions. Soil, sun, fertilizer, mulch, water, crop rotation, plant protection, and garden pests are among the topics discussed in this section. Section two contains profiles of the most nutritious and beneficial foods and herbs. Each profile explains the healing properties and health benefits of the particular plant and gives tips about growing, harvesting, storing, and preparing it. The final section approaches the healing benefits of your garden's products from the standpoint of various conditions and diseases. Whether you suffer from arthritis or want to know how to help prevent heart disease, you'll find the information in this section, which discusses common ailments that may respond to the products of your garden and how to use foods and herbs for maximum results.

Growing a Healing Garden

BEFORE SPRING rolls around and you're anxious to plant, take some time to plan your garden. Even just one evening spent contemplating the greater garden will help you have a successful growing season. The following are all ideas to consider before you make any purchases and before spade meets soil.

CLIMATE Where you live determines what you'll be able to grow in your garden. Ginger, for instance, has considerable therapeutic value, but unless you live in southern Florida or have a greenhouse, you probably won't be able to grow it yourself.

You will also need to consider the hardiness of plants—that is, how tolerant a plant is of cold temperatures. Plants considered hardy are those that can tolerate cold temperatures. These are the kind of plants you'll need to be a successful gardener if you live in a cooler geographical area. Hardy plants can

tolerate cool nights and light frosts, which will allow you to start planting earlier. You'll have to wait to plant tender varieties, however, because they cannot tolerate frost. Many of the profiles in Nature's Bounty, Healing Foods & Herbs, provide information about a plant's hardiness.

Before shopping for seeds or young plants, look through catalogs or inquire at your county's cooperative extension office about varieties that are suitable for your area. Keep a list of them with you so you'll be sure to select plants likely to flourish in your area. Some hardware stores and drugstores may sell plants that won't necessarily grow well in your locale. Although the plants look good at the store, your climate will not support their continued growth.

Gardeners in cooler parts of the country will also need to consider the length of the growing season. Choosing plants and varieties that have a shorter season, meaning they take less time to mature, will almost always guarantee that you'll harvest produce before the first frost. If you live in a warmer area, you can grow almost everything you see in seed catalogs and at local nurseries.

SUNLIGHT REQUIREMENTS As you think about what to grow in your healing garden, you must

consider the sun. Plants capture the sun's vitality and turn it into substances that have health benefits for you. Without adequate sun, plants become leggy and pale and don't produce well. For a plant, lack of sun is a type of starvation.

Too much sun, on the other hand, can be just as damaging. A plant can suffer from sunburn or get scorched. Since it can't protect itself, it may produce seed too early without generating much of a harvest, then wither and die.

What you're aiming for, then, is just the right amount of sun. So watch the sun's path, tracking where shade falls from your house, trees, and bushes. Consider the sun's height in the sky during summer. Determine how many hours your garden plot will be in the sun and how many in the shade.

If your garden will be shaded most of the day, you will be limited in the types of plants you can grow. Vegetables that

produce a fruit, such as squash and pepper, need at least six to eight hours of sun each day, while vegetables that don't make a fruit, such as leafy greens, some root crops, and herbs, do well with partial shade.

Ideally, set up your garden so that all plants are exposed to the cool morning sun. Then arrange plantings so that leafy greens get shade as the hot noon sun sweeps around. Sun-loving plants, such as corn, can get sun all day. You can ensure that plants get the right amount of sun by planting tall crops west of those that need afternoon shade and by taking into account the shade created by trees and buildings.

Also keep in mind that the roots of many trees and bushes extend far beyond their branches. If you're counting on trees or bushes to provide shade, be aware that planting too close to them may be detrimental to their roots. The roots of these trees and bushes may also interfere with digging.

ADJUSTING THE SOIL Plants need food to grow, just as people do. Sun is just one-third of the diet, however. Water and mineral-rich soil make up the other two-thirds of a plant's dietary requirements. Plants make their own vitamins, but they are dependent upon soil for minerals.

To ensure that your plants have a proper soil diet, you need to determine the kind of soil you have in your garden. Soil types vary greatly, from dry, nutrient-poor sand to rich, heavy clay. The texture of the soil is also important. It must be made up of about equal parts dirt (clay, silt, sand) and organic material (decaying plant matter) to allow for air, space for plants' roots, and good drainage. You can add organic material to your garden from your compost pile. If you end up using uncomposted grass clippings, sawdust, or the like, extra nitrogen fertilizer will be needed.

Soil-testing will give you the information you need about the soil. You can opt for a simple soil test kit from the garden store to test the soil's pH—the acid-alkaline balance which is crucial to a plant's health. Or you can do a more detailed soil analysis by sampling the soil and sending it to a laboratory. Detailed tests will give you information about all the nutrients in your soil and the percentage of organic mate-rials it contains in addition to the pH. Check your local nursery, garden store, or county cooperative extension office for complete soil test kits.

Whichever test you use, it's very important to ascertain the pH of your soil because it affects the availability of nutrients. Seven is neutral on the pH scale. Numbers less than seven indicate increasing acidity, and numbers greater than seven reveal increasing alkalinity. Most herbs prefer a pH of 6.5 to 7.0; vegetables prefer a pH between 5.5 and 7.5.

If you don't have access to a soil test kit, you can estimate your soil's pH. Soil tends to be acidic in humid areas or where there are pine and fir trees that drop needles onto the ground. Dry areas tend to have slightly alkaline soil.

Ammonium sulfate is a sulfur product that will move alkaline soil towards neutral. It can be purchased in dry granulated form at a garden store. The soil testing facility will recommend the amount to use.

To adjust acidic soil to a more neutral pH, add ground limestone. The testing facility will usually give recommendations. Otherwise use the boxed guidelines that follow.

SANDY SOIL
4 lbs/100 sq. feet every 2 years
LOAM
6 lbs/100 sq. feet every 2 years
CLAY SOIL
8 lbs/100 sq. feet very 3 years

Turn or till these additives into the soil.

In order to produce healing plants, your garden also needs high levels of phosphorus, potassium, and nitrogen. These essential minerals are found in fertilizer either from organic or inorganic sources. Organic fertilizers come from plant or animal products such as manure, dried blood, bone meal, and fish emulsion. These fertilizers require bacteria in the soil to break them down and make nutrients available to plants. This means that organic fertilizers are not a quick fix, but one you should plan for and use throughout the season and over the years. They are less likely than inorganic fertilizers to burn plants, and they provide a slow release of nutrients over a long period of time. Aged manure is lower in nutrients than other organic fertilizers but improves soil texture due to its bulky organic matter.

Fresh manure should never be used on the garden, as it may contain disease-causing organisms such as *E. coli*, and it is too "hot" (rich in certain substances that can burn plants). Always use old or aged manure that is at least six months old.

Inorganic fertilizers are made synthetically from chemicals. The nutrients in them are instantly available to plants. These kinds of fertilizers usually dissolve quickly in water.

Labels on fertilizers typically have three numbers. The first number tells the percentage of nitrogen (N), the second number the percentage of phosphorus (P), and the third number the percentage of

ORGANIC FERTILIZERS

Fertilizer	N-P-K
Dried blood	13-1.5-0
Kelp	3-22-0
Cottonseed meal	6-2.6-2
Cattle manure	0.5-0.3-0.5
Horse manure	0.6-0.3-0.5
Chicken manure	0.9-0.5-0.8

potassium (K). Most vegetable garden do well with a balanced 10-10-10 fertilizer. If you use organic fertilizers, you may need to mix and match to get a balanced mixture.

It's a good idea to work a balanced fertilizer into the soil as you till the soil and prepare the beds. This gives the plants an immediate boost. Healthy, strong plants are more resistant to diseases and pests, and they tend to produce more and better quality fruits, vegetables, and flowers.

MAPPING IT OUT Once you have decided the best location for proper sunlight, wind protection, and accessibility, draw the plot on paper (graph paper will allow you to draw your plot roughly to scale). Check seed packets to see how far apart

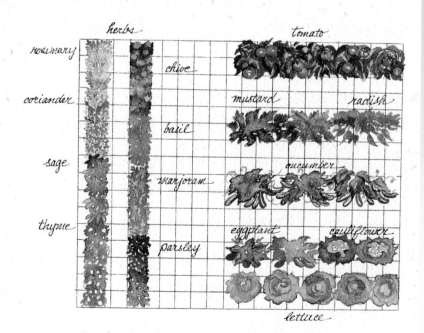

seeds and seedlings need to be planted. Some sprawling plants, such as cucumbers, will take up less room if they are staked on a trellis. Unless you definitely need the shade, put tall plants on the north side of the garden to eliminate unwanted shade on heliotropes, which are plants that particularly love the sun.

COMPANION PLANTING Before assigning all the beds in your plot, consider all the plants you want to grow. Try interspersing plants that mature quickly between plants that mature slowly so that the quick ones are done by the time the slow growers need extra space. Use tall, sun-loving plants to shade those that require shade for part of the day.

Just like people, some plants prefer certain kinds of company to others. If you put plants that like to grow next to one another close to each other, they each seem to produce better and have improved flavor. Some plants emit odors that protect others against certain pests or animals. But for the most part, scientists are not quite sure why some of these relationships work, and indeed, some are not scientifically confirmed. Many speculate that roots or leaves produce excretions that influence the growth of neighboring plants or repel would-be nibblers. Mint, for instance, sends cabbage moths packing, so it's beneficial to plant mint among cabbages. Avoid planting rows of only one kind of crop. A diverse array of plants is attractive and one of the gardener's most effective pesticides and fertilizers. Use the following charts to help you pick good companions.

FAVORABLE COMPANIONS

Vegetables, Herbs, and Flowers

Asparagus	Tomatoes, basil, parsley, calendula
Basil	Tomatoes
Bush beans	Most vegetables, especially cabbage family, carrots, corn, cucumbers, eggplant, peas, potatoes, Swiss chard. Also borage, lovage, marigold, nasturtium, sunflower, oregano, summer savory
Beets	Bush beans, cabbage family, onion, kohlrabi, garlic
Borage	Tomatoes, squash, strawberries
Cabbage family	Beets, celery, cucumbers, lettuce, onion, potatoes, spinach, Swiss chard, chamomile, dill, garlic, hyssop, mint, nasturtium, sage, thyme, pennyroyal, rosemary, lavender
Carrots	Lettuce, leeks, onion, peas, peppers, tomatoes, chives, rosemary, sage, thyme
Celery	Leeks, tomatoes, bush beans, cauliflower, cabbage
Chamomile	Onion, cabbage
Chives	Plant around base of fruit trees—prevents insects from climbing trunk
Corn	Beans, cucumbers, melon, peas, potatoes, squash, pumpkin, marigold, parsley
Cucumbers	Beans, peas, corn, lettuce, radishes, sunflower, marigold, parsley
Dill	Carrots, cabbage
Eggplant	Beans, peppers, marigold, thyme
Garlic	Deters pests, use throughout garden, put near herbs to enhance essential oils, discourages bugs among roses and raspberries
Leeks	Carrots, celery, onion
Lettuce	Beet, cabbage family, carrots, onion, chive, dill, garlic, onion
Marigold	Deters airborne pests and soil nematodes (tiny parasitic worms)
Mint	Tomatoes, cabbage family
Melon	Corn, pumpkin, squash, marigold, nasturtium, oregano

FAVORABLE COMPANIONS

Vegetables, Herbs, and Flowers

Nasturtium	Tomatoes, radishes, cabbage family, cucumbers. Deters aphids and pests, plant throughout garden and under fruit trees
Onion	Beets, cabbage family, carrots, lettuce, peppers, strawberries, Swiss chard, tomatoes, chamomile, dill, summer savory. Protects against slugs and ants
Parsley	Tomatoes, asparagus
Peas	Squash, most vegetables. Contributes nitrogen to soil
Petunia	Protects beans
Peppers	Carrots, eggplant, onion, tomatoes, basil
Potatoes	Beans, cabbage family, corn, eggplant, peas, marigold, horseradish
Pumpkin	Corn
Radishes	A general aid in repelling insects
Rosemary	Deters bean beetles and cabbage moths
Spinach	Strawberries, cabbage family
Squash	Corn, melon, pumpkin, borage, marigold, nasturtium, oregano
Strawberry	Bush beans, spinach, borage
Sunflower	Cucumbers
Tomatoes	Chives, asparagus, carrots, cucumbers, onion, peppers, basil, bee balm, borage, calendula, chive, mint, parsley, marigold, nasturtium
Turnip	Peas
Wormwood	Use as a border, keeps animals out of the garden
Yarrow	Enhances essential oils of herbs

SUCCESSION PLANTING

Remember that you can plant more than one crop of quick-maturing vegetables. An assortment of new lettuce seeds placed in the ground every two weeks will ensure a full salad bowl throughout the growing season. You can also extend your harvest by using varieties that mature at different times. Additionally, quick-maturing cool

UNFAVORABLE COMPANIONS

Beans	Chive, garlic, leek, onion, shallots
Cabbage family	Pole beans, tomatoes
Carrots	Dill
Corn	Tomatoes
Cucumbers	Potatoes, sage
Fennel	Most plants
Onion	Peas, sage
Peas	Chive, garlic, leek, onion, shallot
Potatoes	Cucumbers, squash, tomatoes
Tomatoes	Corn, dill, kohlrabi, potatoes

weather crops planted in the spring can be harvested by early summer, giving up their space to warm-weather crops. As you harvest the heat-loving plants, replace them with plants that can produce into the fall, such as cabbages or root crops. Succession planting allows a large variety of plants to thrive on a small piece of land.

CROP ROTATION If you had a garden in the same location last year, try not to put plants in the same family in the identical place again. Crops need to be rotated yearly or at least every two years to avoid depleting the soil of nutrients important to those plants and to make it more difficult for diseases to get a foothold. Enriching the soil helps prevent this, but it is best to rotate placement. The families that are important to rotate are: cabbage family (broccoli, cauliflower, cabbage, collards, kale, rutabaga, turnips, brussels sprouts, and kohlrabi), cucumber family (cucumbers, squashes, muskmelon, watermelon, and gourds), and the nightshade family (potatoes, tomatoes, eggplant, and peppers).

Be sure to keep accurate records of what you plant, when it's planted, any problems you experience, and the amount of your harvest so you'll have a basis for planning your garden the following year.

SEEDS AND STARTS There are two ways to start plants for your healing garden: seeds and starts. Seeds can be purchased in seed packets or saved from previous plants. Starts are young plants. The purist may want to start everything from seed. And some plants, such as root vegetables, should have their seeds sown directly into the ground because they don't transplant well. However, some seeds such as parsley are difficult and take a long time to germinate, so purchasing a start is best.

Seeds can be started indoors four to eight weeks before the last frost date: Cooler crops can be started closer to eight weeks ahead of time, while warm-weather crops don't like to get too far along, four weeks at most, before being transplanted into warm soil.

You can buy special pots or peat pellets that grow into pot shapes when you water them, or use old egg cartons or cut-off milk containers. Just be sure there is a hole in the bottom for drainage. Clean pots that previously held plants with a mild bleach solution to kill any disease-causing organisms. Put a sterile seedling mix into your containers and dampen it. Follow package directions to determine how deep to plant the seeds. Since they're going to be transplanted later, they can be spaced closer together than recommended for now. Save the seed packets so you can refer to them for spacing instructions later, when you transplant the seedlings into the garden. Keep the seedlings moist in a sunny window until it is time to plant outside. A spray bottle is often the best way to water at first, so as not to displace the seeds. A half-strength fertilizer applied approximately every two weeks will make the young plants thrive. If seedlings stretch toward the light, rotate the container to help them grow evenly. Vegetables to start indoors include: broccoli, eggplant, brussels sprouts, lettuce, cabbage, onion, cauliflower, pepper, celery, squash*, chard, tomato, cucumber*, and watermelon*. (*Start in individual containers so their root systems are not disturbed.)

Young plants started indoors from seed will need to be hardened off, a process in which the plant is gradually accustomed to being out-of-doors. Plants are put out in the sun for a few hours at a time, building up to all day, but need to be brought in at night to avoid cool temperatures. It takes about two weeks for the plants to get used to being outdoors; after that they can be left out overnight if the weather is mild. They are ready to transplant into the ground as long as you don't expect temperatures that are cooler than they can tolerate.

If you decide to begin with purchased starts, choose those that have strong stems and dark green leaves. Ask whether the plants have been hardened off.

Transplanting is easy if your garden soil is already rich and prepared. Decide whether you want to plant in single rows or in "intensive" rows, which are about three feet wide with three rows of planting close to one another. A walkway on either side allows easy access to all plants. This method produces a higher yield and conserves water. To make wide rows, use a rake to pull soil from the path up onto the wide row. Doing this for the entire length of the row, and pulling soil for a path on each side, will create a wide row about four to six inches tall with loose soil just right for young plants. Smooth the top with a rake, then sprinkle three rows of seeds or insert transplants. Each intensive row can have several types of plants.

When placing transplants, dig a hole that will accommodate the plant. Gently pull the plant from its container. Try to avoid touching the stem to prevent damage; instead, handle it mostly by the dirt clump or leaves. If you're using plantable peat pots, break off the top rim of the container so it is level with the ground, otherwise it will wick moisture away from the roots. If roots are compacted, gently pinch off the bottom to encourage new growth. Tomato seedlings are often leggy; if that's the case, remove the lower leaves and plant deep. The tomato's stem will produce roots that will help make a stronger plant. For plants that need a lot of space,

such as melons and cucumbers, make an inverted hill or ridge of soil around the seeds to help hold water while the plant gets established. After transplants are in the ground, pat soil firmly around them, but avoid compressing the area.

MULCHING Mulches help keep down the weed population, insulate the soil, retain moisture, reduce soil erosion and compaction, and if organic mulch is used, eventually contribute to the health of the garden soil. The weather and soil should be warm before mulching so that cool soil temperatures don't stunt root growth. Wait to mulch areas where seeds are planted until the seedlings are well-established, about four inches tall. Transplants can be mulched right away. Arrange a thick layer of mulch, typically about two inches deep, around transplants.

Typical organic mulches include lawn clippings, leaves, sawdust, straw, and wood chips. All of these use up nitrogen as they

Fabric mulches, such as black plastic, are easy to use but must be removed from the garden at the end of the growing season. Fabric is usually better at controlling weeds but can keep too much moisture in the soil if the ground doesn't drain well, resulting in wilting and rotting plants. Fabric mulch is especially helpful if the garden is in an area that was formerly planted in grass; it will keep the rototilled grass from re-establishing itself.

decompose, so either add extra nitrogen or let them decompose up to a year before using. Make sure lawn clippings are dry, or they will rot in the garden. Avoid using walnut leaves or lawn clippings that have been chemically treated, as they contain substances that are toxic to some plants. Keep walnut leaves out of the compost pile, too. Don't use hay as mulch, either, as it contains an enormous amount of weed seeds.

Purchase fabric in wide strips, and cut it into the length of your rows. Bury each side of the fabric in a shallow trench covered with dirt. Slice a three-inch "X" wherever you'll be putting transplants. Dig through the "X," and plant as usual. Water through these holes until plants are established. When the plants are mature enough, you may be able to flood the pathway between fabric-covered rows and let the water soak in, encouraging the roots to reach for it.

MAINTAINING THE HEALING GARDEN

THINNING AND WEEDING When seeds sprout it is important to keep them thinned while they're young. Some gardeners are uncomfortable uprooting plants they have carefully cultivated, but try to squelch those feelings. Poor thinning practices will compromise the quality of all plants and deplete soil resources.

Thin sprouts as soon as possible according to seed package directions. Cut off the unwanted plants at ground level; pulling them out will disturb the root systems of neighbors. For large-seeded plants, wait until seedlings are several inches tall, then choose the best and strongest-looking plant to be master of the mound.

As seeds sprout, it may sometimes be difficult to distinguish between the seedling and the weed you want to destroy. Experience will help you, as does planting in straight rows or mounds. Remember, a weed is simply a plant that is growing in a place you do not want it to grow. Many plants that most gardeners consider to be weeds actually have beneficial properties. As you look through the herb section, you may discover that you're growing many plants that others may consider weeds. Some gardeners recognize beneficial "weeds" and carefully transplant them to their herb garden.

Use a sharp hoe to cut off the tops of weeds as soon as you see them. Persistent weeds may require several clippings before

THE HEALING GARDEN

giving up, at which time their roots die. Try not to pull weeds out by their roots, as this can again disturb the root systems of neighboring plants and may take away large clumps of rich garden soil. Uncontrolled weeds will compete with beneficial plants for light, water, and nutrients. These dreaded garden inhabitants might also harbor insects and disease. It is vitally important to stamp out weeds before they go to seed and scatter their brethren to all parts of your garden. Be consistent and vigilant about weed control so that weeding will only take a minimal amount of time and effort.

NOURISHING THE GARDEN Water is vital to a healthy garden. It provides support for plants' cells and dissolves nutrients in the soil, making them available to roots. Adequate watering is essential to young plants. Water to a depth of six to eight inches to encourage deep rooting. Otherwise shallow roots will develop, making the plant weak (see illustration above). After plants are well-established, the typical garden needs about one inch of water per week. Keep the garden watered well to promote steady growth, which produces the best-tasting fruits and vegetables.

If plants wilt near the end of the day but are recovered by morning, this is not a sign of dryness. During periods of rapid growth the leaves sometimes grow so fast that the roots can't supply them with enough water. However, if plants are wilted in the morning, water is needed.

Overhead watering by sprinkler is not the best method. Wet foliage can set the stage for certain diseases. Instead, water the soil directly. One heavy watering rather than several light ones will encourage deep root growth. Light sprinkling encourages shallow, unhealthy roots. Water in the morning so plants can use the water during the heat of the day and so that any moisture that does get on plants' leaves will evaporate. It's a myth that water on leaves will cause sunburned plants. Watering at night provides a moist habitat for many hours, which encourages certain diseases, molds, and fungus.

About halfway through the growing season you'll need to replace nutrients in the soil. Apply fertilizer about 12–18 inches from the stem of individual large plants or in a four–inch-deep trench alongside a row of smaller plants. Use a moderate amount of balanced fertilizer. Cover the fertilizer with soil and water thoroughly.

PLANT PROTECTION

ASSISTING LARGE PLANTS

Some plants need a little mechanical assistance. Tomatoes do best when staked or caged, while beans or cucumbers love to climb poles. This not only saves garden space, but also keeps leaves and produce off the ground, where they invite disease. Production, too, can be enhanced, as more flowers reach the sun and stems are supported, enabling them to hold heavy produce. Use poles to make tepee shapes or fences, or purchase trellises for vegetables such as beans and peas that put out tendrils and want to climb.

COOL NIGHTS Cold weather can harm young plants, while an early freeze can stop your garden in its tracks. Be aware of the nighttime weather forecast and have some protection on hand to preserve your healing garden when cold weather threatens.

If young plants need protection, cover them. Use inverted milk cartons, plastic jugs or pop bottles with bottoms cut out, or sheets of clear plastic. If using plastic, bury the edges and secure them with rocks. Remove these devices during the day to avoid burning or suffocating plants.

As the season progresses, you may still need to keep alert for frosts, especially if you live at high altitudes. When plants are large, cover them loosely with thin sheets of clear plastic. Apply them while the ground is still warm in the evening, then let the morning sun warm the plants and soil before removing them. The clear plastic makes a kind of instant greenhouse.

PEST INVASION Harmful insects and similar creatures are the bane of every gardener. Check the underside of leaves frequently to make sure there are no unwanted visitors. Keep in mind that not all creatures are harmful—some are simply benign, while others actually deter harmful pests. Check a library or gardening store for books that describe pests and the symptoms they produce. There are numerous methods of prevention, including:

- Choose varieties of vegetables that have been bred to be resistant to pests common to that vegetable. Look for a "V," "F," "N," or "T" on the package.
- Keep plants well watered and well fed. Healthy plants are more resistant to disease and pest invasion.

༯ Remove garden debris quickly.

༯ Intersperse marigolds and nasturtiums throughout the garden; many bugs find the smell of these flowers repugnant. Herbs are helpful too: tansy repels many insects; calendula discourages tomato pests; catnip repels squash beetles; garlic controls aphids, cutworms, and tomato hornworms; thyme fights white flies and cabbage worms; mint wards off aphids, cabbage worms, and beetles.

༯ Import beneficial insects such as ladybugs, praying mantises, and lacewing flies, which can be purchased through garden stores or catalogs. These critters feast on harmful insects.

༯ Use overhead watering only early in the day so plants dry thoroughly before nightfall, when fungi can spread quickly.

༯ Rotate the crops into different areas of the garden each year to prevent plant-specific diseases and pests.

༯ Put a thin ring of cardboard that extends one inch into the soil and one inch above it around transplants of cabbage-family vegetables, peppers, and tomatoes to prevent attacks by cutworms.

༯ Keep plants staked up on poles or trellises so foliage is off the ground.

༯ Try lightweight floating row covers made of fabric such as the brand names Reemay and Agronet.

If unwanted bugs do invade, try these pest control methods that are safe for you and the environment:

༯ Make your own economical and environmentally safe insecticide: To 1 quart of water add 1 tablespoon mild liquid soap with 2 tablespoons rubbing alcohol and $\frac{1}{2}$ teaspoon chili powder. Spray affected plants, making sure to get the underside of leaves. Avoid spraying the actual vegetables, as they can absorb the soap. Spray daily until pests are gone.

ɣ Buy diatomaceous earth and scatter it in the problem area, lightly working it into the top ½ inch of soil. Follow package directions for the amount to use. This powdery substance is derived from one-celled ocean plants called diatoms and is sharp enough to cut and damage the respiratory or digestive systems of insects.

ɣ Beneficial nematodes (tiny parasitic worms) devour other pests. Purchase them in a container at garden stores and mix them into your soil; follow package directions. Most nematodes are unwelcome garden pests, causing knots on stems and roots of plants. However, the variety you purchase will actually help you get rid of bothersome pests.

ɣ Friendly bacteria called *Bacillus thuringiensis* (Bt) paralyze the digestive system of certain pests but do not harm people, birds, honeybees, or helpful insects. Several trade names include Thuricide, Dipel, and B.t. Spray on plants according to package directions.

ɣ To combat slugs and snails, fill jar lids or shallow pans with beer or sugar water with yeast; bury them level with the soil. Slugs are attracted into the pan and drown.

If you decide to use chemical pest control methods, read all labels carefully, follow all directions meticulously, heed warnings, and use as little as possible. If you don't, the chemicals can harm people and animals that wander into the garden. And runoff can contaminate surface waters and, possibly, groundwaters. Try to choose chemicals that are the most environmentally friendly, especially those that won't harm bees needed for pollination or fish if the chemical runs into a stream.

ANIMAL ATTACKS Most gardeners don't mind sharing a little bit of their produce, but animals can wear out their welcome. Sometimes a tall fence of chicken wire is the only way to keep out animal invaders.

To keep birds from eating seedlings, berries, and other succulent items, cover the plants with the same thin floating row covers used to keep out pests. These let in air, water, and light, but make a good barrier.

Moles and gophers might be dissuaded by running water into their holes to fill up and cave in their tunnels. Beer or pop bottles buried so the opening is level with the ground hum when the breeze blows and may keep some of these creatures away. County cooperative extension offices often have traps that can be rented.

Interspersing distasteful plants, such as marigolds and wormwood, can sometimes ward off nibblers, but often they just push past those to find the succulent plants to munch.

HARVESTING YOUR BOUNTY

Stroll through the garden each day to check what is ripe. Items picked too early may not have developed their full taste or all their beneficial substances, but those left on the vine after ripening also diminish in quality, becoming fibrous or tough, and may invite disease if they begin to rot. Harvesting at the appropriate time will encourage plants to keep producing.

Use your senses to determine ripeness. Does it have a deep color? Does it give to slight pressure, if appropriate? Does it have a good aroma? Is it large enough? If you're undecided, pick a small amount, wash, and try it. Harvesting guidelines are given in the food and herb profiles.

It's a good idea to take a basket or some other type of container into the garden to fill with your bounty. Avoid setting produce on the ground so harmful bacteria won't come in contact with it. Be aware that your basket has been sitting in the soil, too, so don't let it contaminate the kitchen counter.

Wash produce with brisk running water. There's no need to use soap or special solutions, and they may not be approved for use on food. Several tablespoons of vinegar in a sink full of water can help neutralize pesticides if chemicals were used in the garden.

Certain produce, such as berries or lettuce, should be washed only when you are ready to use it. Other items may be washed, air-dried, and stored either in a cool place or in the refrigerator. Store tomatoes at room temperature for best flavor. Many vegetables continue to ripen even after they are picked, so try to use them right away or refrigerate to slow the ripening process. The sugar in some vegetables, such as corn and peas, turns to starch quickly unless refrigerated immediately.

PUTTING THE GARDEN TO SLEEP

Perhaps the least rewarding, but one of the most important, gardening tasks is cleaning up debris as plants finish producing and frost blackens leaves. It is imperative to keep the garden space free of debris to prevent bugs and diseases from wintering over, ready to attack tender spring plants. Putting the garden to bed will help it be more successful next year.

Gardens need a blanket—either a cover crop or mulch. Planting a cover crop such as alfalfa, rye, clover, or buckwheat will prevent winter weeds from germinating, limit soil erosion, and contribute nitrogen to the soil. They are relatively carefree and do not require harvesting. You don't need to wait until the entire garden is finished producing. Plant the cover crop as each area of the garden finishes.

To plant a cover crop, clear all debris, then till and smooth the soil. Spread seed, gently rake the surface to work the seed into the top inch of soil, and then tamp lightly. Cover with a light layer of mulch such as straw, then water the area. The crop will nurture your healing garden while it sleeps and can be tilled into the soil in the spring.

If you don't plant a cover crop, consider tilling the entire garden and preparing the soil in the area where you'll start early spring plants. This method may help you avoid waiting out the spring rains to turn or till the garden. In this case, apply thick mulch, as described earlier, to prevent weeds and soil erosion and keep soil from blowing away. Soil preparation for the remaining portion of the garden can wait until spring.

Perennial vegetables such as asparagus and rhubarb need special attention to make it through the winter. As frost kills their foliage, trim the plants down to stubble and cover them thickly with mulch to protect roots from damage. Wait to do this until the soil has cooled; mulching warm soil could cause root rot. Remove mulch as soon as the soil begins to thaw.

it's a good idea to group annual herbs and perennials in different areas.

Herbs are less picky about their growing conditions than their vegetable cousins. Indeed, many of them are considered weeds. In fact, they develop stronger essential oils if grown in moderately dry soil that is not particularly rich in nutrients. A 5-10-10 fertilizer is sufficient. Typically, herbs like a lot of sun—about six hours per day. Some herbs, such as sweet woodruff and violet, will tolerate partial shade.

Many herbs can be grown on a windowsill and can supplement your outdoor herb garden. Your indoor herbs might be those that you use most often in cooking, so they are convenient.

Many herb seeds are difficult to germinate, so gardeners often prefer to start with transplants. Choose healthy looking

YOUR HERB GARDEN

Herbs are beautiful plants with healing properties, and many of them flower. They are extremely easy to grow, as they are not very demanding of soil conditions. Herbs can be grown interspersed among the vegetables in the garden (keep in mind companion plants and pest and disease preventatives), in their own dedicated herb garden, or both. The only herbs that may not be desirable to have in the garden are mints, tansy, and thyme, as they are rampant growers that crowd out other plants. Keep these in containers within the garden or in a contained area. For convenience, plants/seedlings with good color and ample growth. Place them into prepared soil in a hole slightly deeper and wider than the container it comes in. Use about an inch of mulch, then water gently. Slight neglect by the gardener will produce a better crop of herbs, since they tend to like drier conditions. Don't fertilize as often as you do in the garden. If you've inter-mixed plants and herbs in the garden, don't worry about either of these conditions; they will grow, but their essential oils may not be as strong as when conditions are a bit rougher.

Herbs can suffer from pest attacks, just like the vegetables in the garden. Use companion plants to help prevent invasions. Garden stores sell traps for Japanese beetles that like to devour echinacea and basil. Cedarwood incense is said to drive away aphids, whitefly, spider mites, and mealybugs. Stick wands of incense in the herb garden about every 15 feet and light them. You can also follow other preventative and

treatment methods listed in the vegetable gardening section. (See pages 25–27.)

Herbs are best harvested right before blooming, early in the morning after the dew has dried. This is when essential oils are at their peak and flavor is strongest. If you know ahead of time that you'll be harvesting herbs, spray the plant with water the day before to remove dust and dirt, but give the plant time to dry. This is preferable to washing herbs after they have been picked, which can diminish their medicinal properties and flavor. Use sharp scissors, shears, or even fingernails to snip sprigs two to three inches long. Keep future growth in mind and never strip leaves from the growing stem. Fresh herbs store well in the refriger-ator, either in a plastic bag or with their stems in a glass of water (like cut flowers). Harvest herbs for fresh use throughout the growing season. Many perennial herbs such as rose-mary, sage, and thyme like to have their growing shoots snipped frequently. As a general rule, harvest roots in the fall. This is when the plant has stored the most nutrients and healing compounds—its way to prepare for the coming winter.

Wintering over the herb garden is a good way to get a healthy start next spring. Annuals, which last only one season and will need to be planted again, need to be removed, roots and all. Trim back the perennials, getting rid of dead or damaged portions but trimming back healthy growth no more than six inches. Herbs with silver-colored leaves are susceptible to cool temperatures; consider covering them with fabric or evergreen branches. As in the vegetable garden, a cover crop such as buckwheat or rye is advised. If the soil in the herb garden gets quite dry during the winter, apply water. Keep dead branches trimmed off and mulch well arranged.

YOUR FLOWER GARDEN A well-planned perennial flower garden will bring delight throughout the seasons, year after year. Use a book that gives details about perennials: color of blossom, time of blooms, growth characteristics such as spread and height, light, water and soil needs, and color and texture of foliage. One of the tricks in obtaining three seasons of color is to plant under and between—for instance, place spring bulbs under plants that bloom in summer and fall, and summer lilies under plants that bloom in spring and fall. Annuals, especially those with healing properties, can be interspersed in or edge the flower garden.

Plan one step at a time. First list your favorite flowers and find out their characteristics. On paper, map out where you want to place each variety. Then use tracing paper on top of the garden map and determine where bulbs are appropriate. Use more tracing paper to fill in which varieties will bloom during each part of the growing season. Determine whether the garden will look balanced for amount of bloom and color of

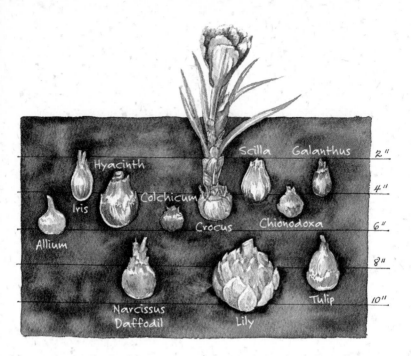

bloom. Be on the lookout to make sure colors don't clash, tall plants don't block shorter ones, and that sun and shade requirements have been met. Remember that mixing foliage colors and textures will help give interest to areas that are not in bloom. Buy enough transplants or apply seed thickly enough that the displays of color will look lush, not sparse.

Some healing flowering herbs, such as hydrangea, St. John's wort, and passion flower are bushes that may be better suited for general landscaping than your flower garden.

CONTAINER GARDENING Even if you live in an apartment, you, too, can have a satisfying garden. All you need is a patio or deck that gets some sunshine. Planting in containers provides flexibility in landscaping and allows you to grow varieties that may not usually be able to tolerate the winters in your area. Containers can be moved into warmer or sunnier areas throughout the day or season. Grouping various types of containers—large, small, tall, short, cute, and functional, some on plant stands and others on the ground, makes an attractive container garden.

Choose pots that complement the plant's characteristics. For instance, a tall plant such as lemon verbena needs a deep pot, while creeping thyme would do well in a wide, shallow pot. To use a decorative pot that has no drainage hole, put a layer of rock in the bottom and insert a clay pot with a drainage hole inside it. Fill the space between the two pots with peat moss. Clay allows soil to dry quickly, so it will need water on a regular basis.

Large containers protect roots from getting too hot on summer days, although small containers are easier to move around. Pots 8–10 inches deep are fine for most vegetables, herbs, and flowers, although tomatoes, peppers, and carrots need a deeper home.

If containers have been used for plants before, discard the old soil and clean the pot with a mild solution of bleach and water. Cover the drainage hole(s) with screen, broken pottery, or even a coffee filter to keep the soil from washing out. If additional drainage is needed, put a layer of pebbles, sand, or perlite in the bottom of the pot. If a pot has no drainage holes, make them near the bottom of the sides, rather than in the bottom, at least ¼ inch in diam-

eter. Fill it with potting soil to within one inch of the top, leaving room for watering. Transplant or seed as normal and water.

Keep in mind that plants growing in containers depend upon you for everything, from fertilizer and nutrients to water and light; they have nowhere else to reach. Container gardens need nourishment on a regular basis. A weak solution of fertilizer, such as fish emulsion, every two to three weeks is recommended.

It is important to let containers dry out thoroughly between waterings to avoid bugs that thrive in damp soil. To determine if watering is necessary, insert a finger two to three inches into the pot's soil. If the dirt feels moist and clings to your finger, then no watering is necessary. If the soil is dry and virtually none clings to your finger, it's

time to water. Always water container plants until it begins to seep out the bottom. Mineral layers can build up in the soil if only partially watered, making it difficult for the plant to thrive. If necessary, use a saucer to catch excess water.

Bush varieties of vegetables are often successful in pots. Or if you have a trellis or strings that dangle from the eaves, tomatoes, peas, beans, and cucumbers can be trained to climb

them. Cherry tomatoes can grow in hanging pots.

Look for weeds and pests, and treat them according to the suggestions on pages 22 and 25–27.

THE INDOOR GARDEN Even if you don't have outdoor space to set containers, you can still grow a small healing garden. Some herbs and vegetables, especially small or bush varieties, grow quite nicely indoors. You just need a sunny window—one that gets four to six hours of direct sun each day.

Prepare containers, and plant seeds or transplants as described in the container garden section. Place in the window and keep moist; a spray bottle may be helpful at first. Be careful not to let the soil dry out. Plants that sit in a sunny window all day have greenhouselike conditions and will use water quickly. Some plants may even need to

be taken out of the window for several hours on particularly hot and bright days. For instance, herbs prefer rooms that are 50°–70°F rather than hot, dry rooms, which may encourage pests and diseases. Rotate containers so that plants don't grow bent as they reach for the sun. Apply a weak solution of fertilizer about every three weeks.

Herbs that enjoy living indoors include basil, bay, calendula, chervil, chives, marjoram, mint, oregano, parsley, rosemary, sage, and scented geranium. Vegetables that you can harvest from the windowsill are those you find in the salad bowl: leaf lettuces, green onions, radishes, and short varieties of carrots.

Nature's Bounty

HEALING FOODS & HERBS

ALLIUM FAMILY

GARLIC, ONIONS, scallions, leeks, and chives are all members of the allium clan, all of which contain potent healing compounds. This profile will only discuss garlic and onions, as they have been studied more than the others.

GARLIC

HEALTH BENEFITS Allicin, a powerful active ingredient in garlic, may help decrease low-density lipoprotein, the "bad" LDL cholesterol, and raise "good" HDL, the high-density lipoprotein cholesterol. This is especially true of fresh garlic, although cooked garlic, too, may also help manage cholesterol. Garlic oil, however, contains very little, if any, allicin and has not been shown to be helpful to the heart in many studies.

Throughout the world, cultures in which a lot of garlic is eaten have less incidence of heart disease than those that do not consume much garlic. This might be attributed to garlic's many antioxidants, which protect arteries from free radical damage and plaque buildup. Numerous human studies show garlic lowers unhealthy cholesterol levels, thereby helping prevent and treat atherosclerosis. It is also helpful for intermittent claudication, or atherosclerosis of the leg veins. It also helps lower mildly elevated blood pressure. Scientists think adenosine, one of garlic's active ingredients, may do this by relaxing tiny muscles that line artery walls, preventing constriction and making it easier for the heart to pump blood through them. The actions of other constituents may also be involved.

Garlic is a proven clot-buster and safer than aspirin for many people. One of its compounds, ajoene, along with other special constituents, helps thin the blood and improve circulation. This makes garlic good at warding off heart attacks and strokes. As little as 1–2 cloves per day, raw or cooked, is all it takes. Luckily, cooking does not destroy ajoene and the other clot-busters; in fact it may help release them. However, cooking does destroy allicin, which may diminish the overall effectiveness of cooked garlic.

In laboratory studies on cells, garlic has shown cancer-fighting ability. Numerous studies have reached the same conclusion: People who eat more garlic are less likely to develop cancer, particularly gastrointestinal forms of cancer. Active ingredients include ajoene, diallyl sulfide, and the flavonoid called quercetin. Ajoene destroys malignant cells while other substances may prod immune cells into attacking cancer more aggressively.

Laboratory studies confirmed that fresh garlic has antibacterial and antiviral properties. (Cooked garlic and garlic oil do not appear to offer this benefit.) In fact, it's able to knock out many common cold and flu viruses, fungi, and yeast. Two small, crushed cloves a day may protect you from the ulcer-causing bacteria *H. pylori*. This in turn may help prevent stomach cancers. Garlic may also help treat *Giardia lamblia*, a parasite from untreated stream water. Although you should see a health professional before self treating if you have an active infection, adding at least 1 crushed garlic clove to ⅓ cup water and drinking the combination two or three times a day for several days may help protect your intestinal tract.

Garlic helps congestion and respiratory problems by triggering fluid-making cells. The additional fluid thins excess mucus. This may be a boon to those suffering from respiratory problems such as asthma, bronchitis, nose and chest congestion, and emphysema.

Unexpected side effects showed up in numerous garlic studies. Many people who ate large quantities of garlic said they felt good emotionally. And participants who suffered from arthritis noticed less joint pain and inflammation.

Some people are allergic to garlic and particularly tend to get an upset stomach when they take it. Otherwise garlic is completely safe.

TYPE OF PLANT Garlic is a hardy perennial that produces a head with bulblets, or cloves.

WHERE TO GROW Garlic needs cool weather during the early stages of growth but doesn't mind heat later on. Plant in an area with loose, fertile soil in full sun.

HOW TO GROW Start garlic from cloves or bulblets, planted with the pointed end up. You can use garlic from the grocery store. Put cloves into the ground about four to six weeks before the date of the last frost. Garlic likes to be slightly dry, especially when reaching maturity; this will improve the flavor.

HARVESTING Harvest garlic bulbs when the tops start to dry out. Dig up the entire plant, and shake off soil. Use the plumpest cloves for cooking and the others for planting.

STORAGE Garlic will keep for several months in a cool, dark, dry place with good air circulation. A small, overturned clay pot is ideal. Check on stored garlic occasionally. If any of the cloves have gone bad, remove them, being careful not to nick the remaining cloves. If cloves begin to sprout they are still useable, although they'll have a milder flavor.

PREPARATION AND SERVING TIPS One of garlic's active ingredients, allicin, is partially destroyed by cooking. For best results, cut, crush, or chop the garlic before using to activate the allicin.

Peel individual cloves, then put through a garlic press for strong flavor, mince for mild flavor, or use whole to impart a hint of garlic.

You can make your own version of fat-free garlic bread by warming a loaf of bread, slicing it lengthwise, then rubbing the inside with a fresh cut clove of garlic. Toast the loaf under the broiler. You'll get a hint of garlic without the fat of traditional garlic bread.

Beware of making homemade garlic oil. Cloves of garlic added to a bottle of oil create the perfect environment for the deadly *Clostridium botulinum* bacteria to flourish. Garlic sometimes carries the bacterial spores from the soil. Either buy commercial garlic-in-oil preparations that contain antibacterial agents such as citric or phosphoric acids or make your own fresh for each use.

Aged garlic extracts are generally comparable to cooked garlic and therefore are not as helpful. If you prefer a pill, use those standardized to 5,000 mg allicin per pill.

ONIONS

HEALTH BENEFITS Although less research has been done on onions than on garlic, findings show the two have many of the same anticancer, cholesterol-lowering properties. A Harvard Medical School study showed that "good" HDL cholesterol climbed significantly when participants ate about half of a medium-sized raw onion each day. Cooked onion did not affect HDL levels.

Like garlic, onions also contain the smooth-muscle relaxant adenosine. This means that onions, too, may fight high blood pressure. They play a role in preventing blood clots as well, keeping blood platelets from sticking together and quickly dissolving clots that may have already formed. Researchers in India found that when raw or cooked onions were eaten along with fatty foods, the blood's clot-dissolving ability remained intact, which doesn't usually occur after fatty foods are eaten. It's a good idea, then, always to include onions when you eat that occasional high-fat meal. Be aware, though, that onions may cause heartburn to worsen in some people.

Onions have many substances that protect you from cancer. Scallions are particularly effective at fighting stomach cancer. Onions are also good at killing bacteria and viruses, which makes them useful for fending off colds and flu.

Studies suggest that the humble onion also helps insulin do its job by decreasing the liver's breakdown of insulin. This is good news for diabetics. Studies in India showed that onions—raw or cooked—help lower blood sugar levels.

This dry bulb from the garden has at least three strong anti-inflammatory agents that may contribute to easing the discomfort of allergies, hay

fever, and asthma by preventing air passages from swelling shut.

TYPE OF PLANT Onions are hardy plants grown as annuals, producing one large bulb per plant. Depending on variety, bulbs will be white, yellow, or red. Long-day onions produce bulbs when grown in the summer months in the North, while short-day onions produce bulbs in the mild winter climate of the South.

WHERE TO GROW Onions prefer cool climates in the early stages of growth and can tolerate frost. Then they need warm weather to produce their bulb. Plant in full sun in an area with rich, fertile soil without rocks or lumps.

HOW TO GROW Onions can be started from sets, which are small bulbs that are dormant, or from transplants or seeds. Seeds are prone to disease and other problems, so they are not rec-ommended.

Small onion sets are better than large ones and are easy to plant. Transplants, however, come in more varieties and are more reliable when it comes to producing a good bulb. Plant sets or transplants about one month before the date of the last frost. Onions like to be moist until near maturity, then they require dry soil. You can tell onions are reaching full growth when tops start to turn yellow, brown, and droopy.

HARVESTING Harvest onions when young for green onions, otherwise wait until the tops dry to harvest the bulbs. Carefully lift the dry bulbs out of the soil.

STORAGE Let bulbs dry thoroughly before storing. "Dry" onions refer to any common onion that does not need refrigeration. This distinguishes them from green onions, which are perishable.

Store dry onions in a dry, dark, cool location with good air circulation. They will keep three to four weeks. Exposure to light makes onions develop a bitter taste. Store onions away from potatoes, which give off a gas that will deteriorate the onions. If onions get warm, they sprout and spoil, but refrigeration also hastens decay. Cut onions should be wrapped in plastic and refrigerated. Use within a day or two.

PREPARATION AND SERVING TIPS Onions are a tasty and healthful seasoning. They are milder when cooked than when raw because the sulfur compounds are converted to sugar when heated. Onions sautée wonderfully, even without butter. Just use a nonstick pan and perhaps a teaspoon of olive oil or even water. Keep the heat low to prevent onions from scorching and turning bitter.

APPLES ARE THE EPITOME of healthy food. The healing substances they contain can help keep cancer at bay, ward off certain bacteria and viruses, and control inflammation, at least according to lab and animal studies. Their fiber helps battle many diseases.

HEALTH BENEFITS Certain substances in apples are adept at preventing inflammation. That means they may help keep open the airways of persons who suffer from asthma and help blood flow smoothly through the vessels of heart disease patients.

Cancer, too, may be thwarted by chemicals in apples. Two phytochemicals, cryptoxanthin and alpha-carotene, are very powerful antioxidants that help keep cells from becoming damaged or mutating—both of which can eventually lead to cancer.

The flesh of an apple is a good source of fiber, especially the soluble type. Soluble fiber works to lower blood cholesterol levels and also helps regulate blood sugar levels. The insoluble fiber in apple peels sweeps the colon clean of substances that can cause irritation and possibly start cancerous growths. It also improves regularity and prevents hemorrhoids and diverticulosis, a condition in which little pockets push out from the wall of the colon. Controlled human studies have shown that apple pectin or water soluble fiber can help cure acute nonbloody diarrhea in children. Pectin was combined with chamomile extract in these studies. You can't substitute apple juice for eating an apple, however; apple juice contains no fiber and is high in simple sugars. It can also cause diarrhea in some susceptible people.

These crisp, crunchy fruits stimulate gums and promote saliva production, making them one of nature's toothbrushes.

TYPE OF PLANT Apple trees are deciduous, typically 15–40 feet tall. Choose a tree according to your favorite eating or cooking apple, disease resistance, and climate.

WHERE TO GROW Apples need full sun and are quite forgiving when it comes to soil—they'll tolerate most conditions except overly wet areas. In order to bloom, apple trees require cool winter nights.

HOW TO GROW Learn how to prune your apple tree so that branches are strong and light can get into the center to produce many apples. If branches get overly heavy with fruit, support them with a pole.

HARVEST Apples are ripe and ready when they come off into your palm with a slight twist and pull. If you have to tug, leave them on the tree. When apples drop to the ground they become bruised and start to decay, so wash and use promptly. WARNING: Always thoroughly wash apples from the ground to avoid contamination from harmful bacteria, especially if using apples raw or in raw cider.

STORAGE Apples need to be refrigerated to keep their crunch. They like a cold, humid environment, so put them in the crisper drawer of the refrigerator. A plastic bag with holes punched in it for ventilation is optimum. Well refrigerated, some varieties will store until spring. Others, such as Golden Delicious, shrivel in a few weeks and get mealy in several months.

PREPARATION AND SERVING TIPS Wash before eating. Dip cut apples in diluted citrus juice to prevent browning. Pack for lunch, or serve baked for breakfast or evening dessert. To keep fat intake to a minimum, try making apple crisp instead of pie.

APRICOTS ARE CHOCK-FULL of beta-carotene and other carotenoids, the beautiful pigments that color fruits and vegetables. There are more than 400 different kinds and most, if not all, are antioxidants. These substances help protect the body from many diseases.

HEALTH BENEFITS Some of apricot's carotenoids such as lycopene, gamma carotene, and cryptoxanthin pack a much more powerful antioxidant punch than does beta-carotene, making them even more useful as cancer-fighters.

Apricots contain some vitamin C, which keeps skin and tissues supple and healthy. Vitamin C also has antioxidant properties and supports the immune system, helping the body make substances to fight off illnesses.

Apricots are rich in fiber for their size, especially soluble fiber. Soluble fiber is the heart-healthy type, lowering blood cholesterol levels and helping people with diabetes maintain stable blood sugar levels. You can count on apricots' insoluble fiber to keep the colon free of toxins and your bowels moving regularly.

Dried apricots, because they are concentrated, are a good source of iron. Three and a half ounces provide about 47 percent of the recommended dietary allowance for men and 31 percent for women.

TYPE OF PLANT Apricots grow on deciduous, broadly spreading trees that reach about 30 feet in height. The tree has pale pink or white flowers in the spring that appear before the leaves. Home fruit trees are easier to tend if they are short; choose trees that

Nature's Bounty
HEALING FOODS & HERBS

ANTIOXIDANTS ABOUND in asparagus. It has substantial amounts of two major antioxidants—vitamins A and C. It is also rich in folate, the B vitamin that has promise for preventing heart disease and even osteoporosis. This vegetable is full of heart-healthy potassium, too.

HEALTH BENEFITS Asparagus is rich in folate (folic acid), the B vitamin that helps prevent the development of neural-tube defects in the fetus during the first trimester. Neural-tube defects are disabling defects in the spinal column. Any woman who might become pregnant needs to load up on folate.

Folate may also play a role in preventing heart disease. It reduces homocysteine levels in the blood. Homocysteine is made during normal body processes, but it can damage artery walls and may also be linked to osteoporosis because it interferes with the proper formation of collagen, which forms the basis of bones. Folate, then, may also play an indirect role in preventing osteoporosis.

Potassium is another nutrient abundant in asparagus—four spears provide nearly as much as half a banana. Potassium keeps the heart healthy and appears to help maintain normal blood pressure.

Asparagus has traditionally been used as a kidney cleanser and diuretic, helping reduce fluid retention. After consuming it, you can observe its tendency to be excreted in the urine by the smell of your urine.

TYPE OF PLANT Asparagus is a 3-foot-tall hardy perennial with fernlike foliage. Its tender, young stems are the edible portion.

WHERE TO GROW Asparagus needs an area that has well-drained soil with a pH higher than 6. It likes full sun and prefers a freezing winter. Asparagus needs a period of dormancy during which the top 2 or 3 inches of soil freezes.

HOW TO GROW Grow asparagus from purchased crowns rather than starting from seed. Plant them about four to six weeks before the average date of the last frost. Dig a trench about 10 inches wide and 10–12 inches deep. Put several inches of soil mixed with organic material in the bottom of the trench. Place the crowns in the trench with roots carefully spread out. Tuck them in with 2 inches of soil on top. As the spears grow, gradually fill the trench with soil. Provide ample water.

HARVEST Crowns develop beneath the soil for the first two years. During the third season, cut off the spears (stems) right below the top of the soil. As the spears regrow, cut them when they are 8–10 inches tall, are bright green, and have compact, closed tips that are slightly purplish. Thick stalks are plump and tender. Avoid stalks that are leafing out—they are past their prime. Stop harvesting spears when they begin coming up pencil-thin.

STORAGE Asparagus is a true cold-lover—even after harvesting. It will keep for almost a week when wrapped loosely in a bag in the refrigerator but will deteriorate quickly if not chilled. For best taste, serve within a day or two of picking. To freeze asparagus, blanch it soon after it is harvested, then wrap tightly in foil or heavy plastic and freeze up to 12 months.

PREPARATION AND SERVING TIPS Wash asparagus carefully to remove sand. Snap off the whitish portion of the stem end, where it breaks easily. Use ends for soup stock. Whether you boil, steam, or microwave asparagus, avoid overcooking it. It will be bright green when cooked crisp-tender.

BEET GREENS ARE PACKED with healing nutrients, including disease fighters such as vitamin A, folate, and potassium. Calcium, too, is available from this nutritional power-house. The variety of vitamins and minerals make these leafy greens an all-around heart-healthy vegetable.

HEALTH BENEFITS If you are trying to quit smoking, beet greens may become your new friend. Just like soil, human blood has a pH value, and a slightly alkaline condition apparently triggers nicotine to stay in the blood longer, reducing the craving for more cigarettes. At the University of Nebraska Medical Center, researchers found that beet greens push blood pH slightly toward the alkaline side. Smokers who are trying to quit might try eating plenty of alkaline foods to reduce their need for nicotine. Other high-alkaline foods include dandelion greens, spinach, and raisins.

Beet greens are abundant in folate. This B vitamin protects lung cells from damage that can trigger cancer, so smokers get a double dose of prevention from these greens. Folate helps fight heart disease and osteoporosis by curbing homocysteine levels. It also helps prevent certain birth defects when the mother gets sufficient amounts of it early in her pregnancy.

These healing garden greens are loaded with vitamin A, which comes mostly from beta-carotene and its carotenoid cousins. The carotenoids form a strong anticancer team. Vitamin

C, another antioxidant, is present in good quantities as well.

Beet greens are also loaded with potassium, which helps lower high blood pressure and normalize an irregular heart beat.

A respectable source of calcium, beet greens support bones. However, like spinach, they contain oxalic acid that binds up the calcium.

TYPE OF PLANT A hardy root crop with large, edible leaves.

WHERE TO GROW Beets prefer cool climates and can tolerate frost. They grow well during the winter in southern parts of the country.

HOW TO GROW Plant several weeks before the average date of the last frost in loose soil rich in organic matter; they dislike acidic soil. Beet seeds come in small clusters about the size of a pea; plant them directly into the garden. Several seedlings will sprout from each cluster. Thin the sprouts 2–3 inches apart once true leaves have developed. Beets have high water and potassium needs.

HARVESTING Eat thinned seedlings as a raw salad green. After roots have developed into beets, trim the tops about two inches from the base. Greens should be crisp and dark green; small leaves have the best flavor.

STORAGE Refrigerate beet greens in a plastic bag to help them retain nutrients. They wilt if kept more than several days. A dip in ice water may help to revive them if they do wilt.

PREPARATION AND SERVING TIPS Wash greens thoroughly to remove sand. Use small, tender leaves in salads. Steaming is the best cooking method to preserve the rich array of nutrients in beet greens. A splash of lemon juice or seasoned vinegar plus herbs makes them tasty— or mix them with cooked, diced beets. Beet greens also boost the nutritional value of soup, as does the cooking liquid left after steaming them, while adding flavor.

BEET GREENS

52 THE HEALING GARDEN

BEETS HAVE LONG BEEN valued for their rich flavor, sweet taste, and vital nutrients. Some people, however, are concerned about the red color they see in their urine and stool a few days after eating beets. Although alarming, the color is harmless red pigment that some people are unable to break down.

HEALTH BENEFITS Beets are particularly rich in the B vitamin folate, which is essential for preventing a certain type of anemia and birth defects that affect the spinal column. Folate may prevent cancer, too, by protecting the DNA in cells from damage and mutation. Mutated cells are often the beginning of cancerous cells.

Beets contain a wealth of soluble and insoluble fiber. The insoluble fiber helps promote bowel movements, keeping the intestines toned. The soluble fiber helps sugars absorb slowly, thus stabilizing blood sugar levels. Of course, soluble fiber promotes lowered blood cholesterol levels, too.

Packed full of potassium, beets keep the heart beating regularly and may help to normalize high blood pressure.

TYPE OF PLANT Beets are a hardy annual grown for bulbous roots and leafy greens. There are red and golden varieties.

WHERE TO GROW Beets are a cool-climate vegetable, tolerating frosts well. In warm climates they need additional water and mulching, or better yet, grow them as fall and winter crops. Beets prefer loose, rich soil, and they need about six hours of sun each day.

HOW TO GROW Sow seeds about one month before the last frost, and continue seeding every two weeks until midsummer for successive crops. The seeds are in a paperlike husk that should be soaked overnight before planting. Thin beets once the true leaves appear, so they are spaced 2–3 inches apart. This vegetable requires a good supply of potassium and water. Beets grown in warm climates can become woody if the weather gets hot, so harvest them before the hot weather.

HARVEST Dig beets when their roots get about 1½ –3 inches in diameter, typically 60 to 80 days, depending on the variety. Flavor will diminish if they are left in the ground after maturity. Pull the beets up gently, trying not to disturb neighboring plants.

STORAGE Once harvested, immediately cut off the greens to prevent moisture loss from the beet. Leave 2 inches of stem to prevent the beet from "bleeding" when it's cooked, and leave the taproot intact. Beets should be kept in a cool spot, and if refrigerated will keep for a couple of weeks.

PREPARATION AND SERVING TIPS
Wash fresh beets gently to avoid breaking the skin and allowing color and nutrients to escape. Microwaving may be the cooking method of choice to retain the most nutrients. Steaming is acceptable, too, but it takes 25 to 45 minutes. Beets are done when pierced easily with a fork. The highest concentration of nutrients is just under the skin. Beets' powerful pigment will stain utensils and wooden cutting boards—wet them first to minimize staining.

Beets contain more sugar than starch, giving them a sweet taste well suited to being served cold, warm, or room temperature. Cooked beets are delightful with herbed butter or olive oil, salt, and pepper. Borscht, a popular cold soup, is made from beets.

BLUEBERRIES, BLACKBERRIES, raspberries, and strawberries contain plant chemicals such as flavonoids that promote health in a variety of ways. They are also loaded with vitamin C, potassium, and fiber.

HEALTH BENEFITS Catechins are plant chemicals called polyphenols. They are excellent antioxidants that are especially prized for battling heart disease and cancer in the digestive tract. Other polyphenols in berries are special antioxidants, too, preventing cancerous nitrosamines from forming in the stomach and intestines. Some Russian studies show that berries can prevent heart disease. Human studies are lacking to show if berries prevent cancer.

Berries are rich sources of flavonoids, substances that contribute their striking colors to the fruits and health benefits to you. They promote elasticity of blood vessels.

Ellagic acid, another potent natural substance found in berries, may help prevent certain types of cancer. It is able to withstand heat, so cooked berries or jam can still provide this valuable substance.

Although yet to be proved in clinical studies, blueberries are believed to fight bladder infections in much the same way that cranberries do—making the walls of the bladder and urinary tract so slippery that bacteria cannot survive there.

TYPE OF PLANT Berries are perennials that spread easily. Strawberries are productive for two to three years. Blackberries and raspberries produce fruit for ten years or more. Blueberries produce indefinitely.

WHERE TO GROW Raspberries and strawberries like well-drained soil, whereas blackberries and blueberries tolerate moderately moist conditions. All berries require full sun. Plant berries where yearly tilling will not interfere with their root systems.

HOW TO GROW Most berries don't produce much of a crop for the first year or two. Blueberries require more than six years to reach maximum production. Raspberries, blackberries, and blueberries require high levels of fertilizer; strawberries need only a moderate level with a low nitrogen content. Water the berry patch faithfully.

HARVESTING Strawberry patches need to be picked at least every other day, in the morning while berries are cool. Berries should be fully red. Raspberries are ready when they come off the stem easily, regardless of their color. Blackberries often look ripe when still sour; they must be completely black and soft before picking. Taste blueberries to determine ripeness. They should be dark purplish-blue with a dusky, whitish "bloom;" firm; and plump. Harvest blueberries weekly.

STORAGE Pick through harvested berries to remove those that are overly soft, moldy, crushed, or shriveled. Refrigerate immediately in a dry, covered, nonmetal container, without washing first. Blueberries will keep about a week, strawberries for several days; blackberries and raspberries only hold for about one day. To freeze, wash carefully, drain until dry, then freeze in a single layer on cookie sheets. Transfer to resealable plastic bags.

PREPARATION AND SERVING TIPS Wash berries thoroughly just before using. Enjoy them plain or added to cereal or baked goods. Add any of the berries to yogurt and juice and whiz in a blender for a refreshing smoothie.

CARROTS

MODERN SCIENCE HAS DETERMINED that carrots do much more than help eyesight. They offer a natural defense against heart disease, strokes, cancer, cataracts, and even constipation. And it only takes one carrot a day to dramatically reduce health risks.

HEALTH BENEFITS Studies show that a humble carrot a day reduced the risk of heart attack in women by 22 percent, and a carrot a day five days per week reduced women's stroke risk by 68 percent. Women who did have a stroke were less likely to die or be disabled. Scientists believe that phytochemicals (plant chemicals) in carrots protect oxygen-deprived brain cells.

Lung cancer risk plunged by 60 percent in a different study when a carrot was eaten twice a week. The incidence of other cancers, such as stomach, mouth, and those of the female reproductive tract, are also decreased by eating carrots.

One raw carrot or ½ cup cooked carrots supplies two to three times the recommended daily intake of vitamin A in the form of protective beta-carotene. Carrots contain other carotenoids that are even more potent cancer warriors than beta-carotene: alpha-carotene, gamma-carotene, lycopene, and lutein.

Carrots are equally rich in soluble and insoluble fiber. The soluble type works in your blood, while the insoluble type works in the colon.

TYPE OF PLANT Carrots are biennials, often grown as annuals, which come in many varieties.

WHERE TO GROW Cold climates make carrots feel at home.

Raised beds offer the ideal loose, deep, and rock-free soil carrots need to thrive.

HOW TO GROW Carrots germinate slowly, taking up to three weeks. To prevent a hard crust of soil forming before young shoots push through, intersperse radish seeds with the carrot seeds. As the radishes sprout, they'll keep the top of the soil crumbly. Plant every two or three weeks for a continuous crop. If temperatures are hot, use mulch to keep soil cooler.

HARVEST After the growing time specified for the variety you planted, pull up a test carrot. Make sure the ground is moist so as not to break the root. Carrots are ready if they have full color and appropriate length. Carrots can stay in the ground for about three weeks after maturity. Carrots that were planted to mature in fall or winter may need mulch to prevent freezing while they finish maturing.

STORAGE Clip off carrot greens to preserve moisture in the carrots. Carrots will keep for several weeks in perforated plastic bags in the crisper drawer of the refrigerator. Avoid storing carrots next to apples or pears, which produce ethylene gas that will cause the carrots to spoil.

PREPARATION AND SERVING TIPS Thoroughly wash and scrub carrots to remove soil contaminants. Scrubbing rather than peeling preserves nutrients. However, if pesticides were used in the garden, peel the carrots and trim the top end.

Raw, grated carrots can compliment a salad or be the main attraction—add chives and chervil with raspberry vinegar and olive oil for a light salad.

The nutrients in lightly cooked carrots are more usable by the body than those in raw carrots. Steaming is the best cooking method. The soluble fiber in cooked, puréed carrots adds thickness to foods such as soups and sauces, replacing butter and cream. Carrot juice, however, contains no fiber.

CELERY IS NOT JUST a simple diet food. New research links it to blood pressure reduction. Celery also holds promise in preventing certain types of cancer.

HEALTH BENEFITS Asian cultures have used celery as a remedy for high blood pressure for thousands of years. Now researchers at the University of Chicago are confirming this health benefit. Celery seed is loaded with a phytochemical called 3-N-butyl phthalide, which is able to lower blood pressure. When researchers gave rats with high blood pressure the amount of 3-N-butyl phthalide normally found in 3 or 4 stalks of celery, their blood pressure dropped dramatically. The researchers theorize that celery may reduce stress hormones that constrict blood vessels, suggesting it might be most effective for those whose high blood pressure is due to mental stress.

The National Cancer Institute is looking into celery, too. It appears that celery may help prevent stomach cancer.

Although many people believe that celery is high in sodium, it really isn't. It contains merely 35 mg of sodium per stalk. To put this in perspective, our bodies only need about 200 mg per day, and the upper recommended daily limit for sodium is 2,400 mg. A 1-cup serving of canned soup often has more than 1,000 mg.

Celery does not contain "negative calories" either. You do not burn more calories chewing it than it provides—which is a mere 6 calories per stalk.

Celery is a diuretic and is traditionally used to treat osteoarthritis and gout. The seeds have a stronger effect than the stalk. While animal studies have confirmed the diuretic and anti-inflammatory activities of celery seeds, no clinical studies have generally confirmed the efficacy of celery for these conditions. The exceptions are studies in India and Australia that used celery seed to effectively treat osteoarthritis.

TYPE OF PLANT Celery is a hardy biennial that is grown as an annual. Its stalks, leaves, and seeds are edible. Pascal is the most common variety.

WHERE TO GROW Celery prefers cool climates, especially cool nights. In northern climates, plant transplants several weeks before the last frost. In southern areas, plant it in late summer. Celery likes moist conditions and rich, well-draining soil.

HOW TO GROW Celery is considered difficult to grow; its seeds may take two to three months to germinate. Celery plants require a lot of water and fertilizer. If exposed to the sun, celery becomes very bitter. Blanch the plants by piling soil up around the stems, and plant seedlings about 8 inches apart so the foliage can shade the stalks.

HARVESTING Celery matures slowly, taking three to four months. Stems should be compact and glossy, topped by fresh, green leaves. Harvest before the first hard frost by cutting at or slightly below the soil line.

STORAGE Celery will keep for a week or two in a plastic bag in the refrigerator. Occasionally sprinkle with water to avoid wilting. The stalks should feel firm and crisp; discard those with bruises, cuts, or soft and darkened spots.

PREPARATION AND SERVING TIPS Remove stalks only as needed. Scrub well to remove the soil lodged in the ridges. Trim off the whitish base end. A ten-minute ice water bath will perk up limp celery.

Use as snacks, in salads or soups, or braised with onions. Put seeds in soup or grind them and sprinkle over your dish.

CITRUS FRUITS

ORANGES, GRAPEFRUITS, lemons, limes, and their cousins, such as mandarins and tangerines, contain many powerful anticancer substances and flavonoids. They are also rich in vitamin C, folate, and soluble fiber.

HEALTH BENEFITS Limonene, one of the many cancer-fighting phytochemicals in these fruits, is unique to citrus. It urges the body to produce glutathione enzymes that attack and destroy cell-damaging free radicals.

Albedo, another name for the white membrane on the outside of the peeled fruit, is often stripped and tossed away in disgust. But albedo is actually one of the most beneficial portions of the citrus fruit. It contains precious flavonoids, substances that strengthen blood vessels and capillaries, improving their elasticity and thus preventing breakage and bruising. The albedo is also rich in soluble fiber, the type that helps lower blood cholesterol levels.

One piece of citrus fruit meets or exceeds the daily requirement for vitamin C. An antioxi-dant, this vitamin prevents nitrates from turning into cancer-causing nitrosamines. Vitamin C is essential for maintaining collagen, the "glue" in bones, muscles, and tendons that holds us together.

Citrus fruits, especially oranges, often cause allergies, particularly in young children. Wait until your child is at least one year old and watch carefully for allergic reaction when first introducing citrus into the diet.

Note: Gardening tips for citrus fruits can be found at the end of this profile.

ORANGES

In addition to the beneficial properties described above, oranges are also rich in potassium, the mineral that wards off blood-pressure problems, and in folate, which fights heart disease and prevents certain birth defects. There's even a bit of calcium in an orange.

Oranges and tangerines contain beta-cryptoxanthin, an antioxidant similar to beta-carotene. Researchers speculate that this phytochemical may help reduce the risk of stomach and pancreatic cancer.

Chinese medicine uses dried orange peel to aid digestion and purge excess water from the body. Orange essential oils are used in aromatherapy to alleviate anxiety and nervous depression. Its fragrance is said to convey a positive feeling. However, research is lacking to substantiate these claims. Rubbed on skin, citrus oil stimulates circulation and may help acne and calluses.

GRAPEFRUIT

Pink and red grapefruit are good sources not only of beta-carotene but also another carotenoid called lycopene. Lycopene is twice as powerful an antioxidant as beta-carotene. Scientists have linked higher intake of lycopene to a decreased incidence of prostate cancer, although higher intakes of grapefruit have not been so specifically linked.

Grapefruit's inner white membrane contains a good dose of a special soluble fiber called galacturonic acid. This compound may help decrease atherosclerosis by lowering cholesterol levels.

Grapefruit is full of powerful phytochemicals such as flavonoids, terpenes, coumarins, and limonoids, all of which protect cells.

Grapefruit and especially its juice enhance the absorption of and change how the body processes certain prescription drugs. Drugs of particular importance are coumadin, cyclosporin, calcium channel blockers for high blood pressure, some antihistamines, and some cholesterol-lowering drugs. To avoid getting more medication than intended, tell your doctor how much and how often you typically eat grapefruit or drink its juice.

Specialists in aromatherapy state that grapefruit essential oil triggers certain brain chemicals that give a slight feeling of euphoria and combats depression. Some believe it is useful in treating eating disorders. Clinical studies have not substantiated these claims.

LEMONS

Lemon oil is antiseptic. Used in aromatherapy diffusers, it may kill airborne germs. Research shows that it stimulates the mind while improving concentration and memory. People often use it while working at their desks. The light scent may uplift a dreary mood.

Used on the hair, lemon oil may help diminish dandruff and oil. It cleanses and tones oily skin and soothes infected cuts and insect bites. Applied directly to open wounds, lemon oil may sting. Be careful, as lemon oil increase sensitivity to the sun.

LIMES

LIMES Like other citrus oils, lime may battle depression and bring a feeling of well-being. It also may alleviate exhaustion. A few drops taken internally may reduce unwanted gas. Lime oil is noted to have antiseptic properties and may prevent infections. It is a good skin toner, but can increase sensivity to the sun.

GARDENING TIPS

TYPE OF PLANT Citrus are small evergreen trees that are typically less than 15 feet tall. The scented blossoms give way to fruit that stays on the tree for long periods of time.

WHERE TO GROW Citrus trees need a warm climate to ripen their fruit, but some varieties tolerate frost for short periods.

HOW TO GROW Citrus do well in most types of soil, except for wet areas. They require full sun. Dwarf varieties can be grown in containers. Make sure the soil is well drained and that the plants receive adequate fertilizer.

HARVESTING It takes nearly a year for citrus fruits to ripen, depending on the variety. Richness of color determines ripeness, along with heaviness. Fruits are ready to harvest when they come off the tree with a twist and slight tug. If left on the tree after maturity, citrus fruits may begin to regreen, which is the development of a harmless green tinge around the stem end of the fruit.

STORAGE If refrigerated loose in the vegetable crisper, citrus fruits keep well. Lemons and limes will store for up to two weeks, oranges for about three weeks, and grapefruit up to a month. At room temperature the fruits may shrivel or mold after one to two weeks.

PREPARATION AND SERVING TIPS
Wash before cutting to avoid transferring harmful bacteria on the peel to the inside of the fruit. Scrub lightly with a vegetable brush to clean the small indentations of the peel. Citrus taste sweeter and give more juice when at room temperature.

Choose seedless navels for fresh eating or salads. Use Valencias for juice.

For breakfast, sprinkle a little brown sugar on a grapefruit half and broil until it bubbles. Try substituting grapefruit juice for orange or lemon in citrus vinaigrette dressing.

Lemon and lime juices perk up steamed vegetables, salad dressings, and even soups.

RESEARCHERS HAVE STUDIED cruciferous vegetables extensively because of their ability to prevent cancer. Several servings a week of these vegetables will greatly reduce cancer risk.

There are many members in the cruciferous, or cabbage, family. They include broccoli, cabbages, cauliflower, collards, kale, mustard and turnip greens, brussels sprouts, kohlrabi, rutabagas, radishes, horseradish, and turnips.

Note: Gardening tips for the cruciferous family can be found at the end of this profile.

BROCCOLI

HEALTH BENEFITS

Broccoli is a nutrient-dense food. It's packed full of vitamins and minerals, yet doesn't have many calories. This attractive vegetable is a great source of vitamins C, A, and folate. It is also a good source of the minerals chromium and calcium. It's rich in fiber as well. The antioxidants and nutrients in broccoli help reduce the risk of heart disease and several kinds of cancer. But that's not all broccoli can do. It contains a host of other antioxidants including quercetin, glutathione, and lutein that squash the free radicals that contribute to the development of cancer.

In addition, broccoli and its cousins naturally contain cancer-protective phytochemicals such as indoles; sulforaphane, which is an isothiocyanate; and glutathione. Some of these substances rid the body of extra estrogen, reducing the risk of estrogen-related cancers such as breast cancer.

Broccoli is a rich source of insoluble and soluble fiber. As a result, this favorite vegetable helps prevent constipation, hemorrhoids, diverticular disease, and colon cancer, as well as diabetes, heart disease, and obesity.

New research shows that broccoli sprouts are very high in anticancer nutrients.

Eating large amounts of cruciferous vegetables may make hypothyroidism worse in those who have this condition.

STORAGE For best flavor and nutrient retention, keep broccoli refrigerated in a plastic bag in the vegetable crisper. Unrefrigerated, broccoli decomposes, making it woody and fibrous.

PREPARATION AND SERVING TIPS
Some of broccoli's protective phytochemicals are destroyed by excessive heat, so it is best eaten raw or lightly cooked. Wash carefully just before eating or cooking. Peel the stems as you would a carrot and trim the ends. Stems and leaves are full of nutrients too; dice them for soup. To help the stems cook at the same rate as the more delicate head, make several cuts through them. Steam briefly, maintaining a crisp-tender texture and bright green color. To avoid unpleasant cooking odors, don't cover the pot for the first few minutes of cooking to let the sulfur fumes escape.

CABBAGE

HEALTH BENEFITS
Cabbage juice has been used to prevent and heal ulcers for more than 40 years. Current research at the Stanford University School of Medicine revealed that when ulcer patients drank

1 quart of raw cabbage juice each day, ulcers in the stomach and small intestine healed in about five days. People who ate cabbage instead of drinking the juice also had faster healing times than those who did not eat cabbage.

Cabbage accomplishes this by killing bacteria, including the ulcer-causing *H. pylori*. Secondly, it contains a phytochemical called gefarnate that coaxes stomach cells into making extra mucus, which protects the stomach wall from digestive acid.

As a cruciferous family member, cabbages of all types help fight the war on cancer. Two types of darker-colored cabbage—savoy and bok choy—also provide beta-carotene.

SELECTION AND STORAGE Store cabbage, whole, in the crisper drawer of your refrigerator. Compact heads keep for a couple of weeks if uncut. Leafy varieties should be used within a few days.

PREPARATION AND SERVING TIPS Discard outer leaves, cut into quarters, and wash. Leave the core in to hold the leaves together, and steam lightly. If using raw, cut as close to serving time as possible to retain vitamin C.

To make cabbage juice, process with a juicer. If the taste is too strong, add carrot juice for sweetness.

CAULIFLOWER

HEALTH BENEFITS As a cruciferous vegetable, cauliflower is a natural cancer fighter. It is also notable for its vitamin C levels.

Cauliflower is a respectable source of fiber, folate, and potassium, proving it's more nutritious than its white appearance suggests.

SELECTION AND STORAGE Store cauliflower unwashed, uncut, and loosely wrapped in a plastic bag in the refrigerator crisper. Keep upright to prevent moisture from collecting on the surface, which may lead to brown spots. Cauliflower will keep about two to five days.

PREPARATION AND SERVING TIPS
Remove outer leaves and gently break off the florets. Wash well and trim away brown patches.

Cauliflower serves up well both raw and cooked, although its flavor is less intense when raw. Serve raw with dip or in marinated salads.

Steam lightly to preserve nutrients and flavor. As with other cruciferous vegetables, use a non-aluminum pan with no lid at the beginning of cooking.

COLLARD GREENS

HEALTH BENEFITS Collards practically overflow with vitamin A, mostly in the form of beta-carotene. The outer leaves usually contain more of this nutrient than do the inner leaves. Other carotenoids in collards, called lutein and zeaxanthin, provide extra cancer protection.

Collard greens contain hormone-regulating indoles. When experts at the University of Nebraska fed collards and cabbage to mice, they not only had a lower rate of cancer, but the cancer was prevented from spreading.

Collard greens are high in oxalates, which bind calcium into unabsorbable complexes. People who are prone to kidney stones need to limit their intake of high-oxalate foods.

STORAGE Store collards unwashed in a damp paper towel sealed in a plastic bag. They will keep four to five days. Wash well before cooking, since most greens have dirt clinging to their leaves.

The flavor of the leaves is relatively mild compared to most other greens. Remove the tough stems, and cook only the leaves uncovered in a small amount of water to preserve the vitamin C. Use the cooking liquid for soup to benefit from the nutrients that leach into the water. For a vegetable side dish, simmer in seasoned water or broth for up to 30 minutes.

KALE

HEALTH BENEFITS Kale is one of the most nutritious of the greens. It's a great source of vitamin A in the form of beta-carotene and has more lutein than any other vegetable that's been analyzed. It's rich, too, in zeaxanthin, another antioxidant carotenoid.

Kale is also a great source of potassium and absorbable calcium. And of course, since it's part of the cruciferous tribe, it most likely has all the wonderful anticancer characteristics discussed in the broccoli and cabbage profiles. This has not yet been confirmed as relatively little research has been done on kale.

STORAGE Wrap fresh kale in damp paper towels; store in a plastic bag in the refrigerator. Use within a few days; the flavor gets stronger the longer it is stored.

PREPARATION AND SERVING TIPS Wash thoroughly before cooking. Try simmering the greens in a well-seasoned stock or broth, just until tender; leafy greens cook down a great deal.

MUSTARD GREENS AND TURNIP GREENS

HEALTH BENEFITS These greens are overflowing with lutein, beta-carotene, and zeaxanthin; they are relatively rich in iron and well-absorbed calcium. They also have significant levels of potassium and vitamin C.

STORAGE Store in a plastic bag in the refrigerator. They will keep unwashed up to three days. Storing longer intensifies the flavor.

Wash thoroughly and trim or remove ribs and stems. Steam until just wilted.

GARDENING TIPS

TYPE OF PLANT Cruciferous vegetables are hardy plants, grown as annuals.

WHERE TO GROW This family prefers cool conditions, but can thrive almost anywhere if it doesn't get hot for long periods. They even tolerate frost. Fertile, well-drained soil is preferred.

HOW TO GROW Cruciferous vegetables can be planted from transplants several weeks before the last frost date. If transplants are leggy, plant deep to grow a stout plant. Long stretches of cold or hot weather will make these plants bolt, which means they go to seed before producing a head. Cruciferous vegetables are best grown in early spring and early fall, when temperatures are mild and there is no threat of heat.

Kale prefers growing in the fall and will last through the winter in many areas. Frost even improves its flavor. Ample water is especially important to the root vegetables of this family such as rutabagas and turnips to keep them from becoming woody and strong flavored. Cauliflower sunburns easily. To prevent this, tie several of the plant's leaves over the top of the white head as a cover when it is about the size of a tennis ball.

HARVESTING Cut broccoli heads off with 5–6 inches of stalk remaining. Harvest before small yellow flowers start to appear.

To harvest cabbage, cut the well-developed head off at ground level. When cauliflower has reached the appropriate diameter, cut the head off the main stem.

Kale doesn't mind staying in the garden until needed, but don't let it wait so long that it gets tough. Like kale, collard greens improve in flavor after experiencing a frost, but pick before a hard freeze by clipping off lower leaves first. Pick greens of turnips when young and tender.

MELONS COME in a wide variety of shapes, sizes, and flavors, yet have certain healing nutrients in common. Their high levels of potassium benefit the heart. Some melons have health-boosting phytochemicals and top-notch amounts of vitamins C and A.

HEALTH BENEFITS Orange-fleshed melons, such as cantaloupe, are high in beta-carotene. One cup of melon cubes supplies nearly everyone's daily requirement for vitamin A. When studying endometrial cancer, researchers at the University of Alabama reported that women who did not have this cancer had eaten at least one food high in beta-carotene, such as cantaloupe, every day. The women who had endometrial cancer had eaten less than one beta-carotene food per week.

Watermelon's red pulp is teeming with a different carotenoid, lycopene. Lycopene is even more potent than beta-carotene at doing away with free radicals, those dam-

aging molecules that can be the culprits in heart disease, cancer, and cataracts. High intakes of lycopene, though not watermelon itself as yet, are linked to a decreased incidence of prostate cancer.

TYPE OF PLANT Melons are annuals that belong to the cucumber family. They grow as large, spreading vines. Melons commonly called cantaloupe are actually muskmelons. Honeydew and watermelon are two other successful garden melons.

WHERE TO GROW Melons love long, hot summers and do not tolerate frost. Plant melons in an area where they can spread up to 6 feet in diameter.

HOW TO GROW Plant seedlings several weeks after all danger of frost has passed, when the soil is warm. Put several seeds in an inverted mound, thinning to the strongest two or three plants. If starting with transplants, use peat pots to avoid disturbing the roots when putting them into the garden. Plant different types of melons far away from one another and away from cucumbers and squashes to avoid cross-pollination.

Melons demand a lot of water and nutrients. They need full sun and well-draining soil.

HARVESTING Let melons ripen on the vine, at which point they will easily detach from their stem. When ripe, muskmelons will be fragrant, honeydew's rind will be slightly yellowish and sticky, and watermelons will have a yellowish underside and sound hollow when tapped.

STORAGE Mature musk- and honeydew melons will continue to ripen off the vine, so eat or refrigerate quickly. Watermelons do not continue to ripen after being picked, so they will store for a week or so, longer if refrigerated. After cutting any melon, leave the seeds in place to retain moisture. Cover with plastic wrap and refrigerate. Cut melons should be eaten as soon as possible, since the flesh tends to deteriorate rapidly and become slimy.

PREPARATION AND SERVING TIPS Wash all melons thoroughly before cutting to prevent the knife from carrying harmful bacteria to the inside of the melon. Of course, melons are great eaten alone or in fruit salads, but consider making smoothies out of them or even cool, refreshing fruit soups.

Some people prefer to eat melons alone or not at all to avoid digestive problems. If melons give you discomfort, try eating them between meals rather than with meals.

NIGHTSHADE VEGETABLES

THE NIGHTSHADE (solanaceae) family includes eggplant, sweet and hot peppers, tomatoes, and potatoes. Each member has its own "active ingredient" that promotes health. Although some arthritis sufferers get relief by avoiding this family, others do not. Scientists have been unable to find a chemical culprit.

EGGPLANT

HEALTH BENEFITS Eggplant is rich in potassium but not in other minerals or vitamins. However, it does contain the phytochemicals of the class polyphenols and monoterpenes, which have antioxidant properties and trigger the activity of enzymes that protect against cancer.

X Eggplant, peppers, and tomatoes all have similar growing requirements, which are discussed following the tomato profile.

STORAGE An eggplant likes temperatures of about 50 degrees but can be stored in the refrigerator's crisper for several days. Be gentle; it bruises easily. Brown or tan patches or scars are signs of decay.

PREPARATION AND SERVING TIPS
Wash the eggplant, then cut off the cap. Use a stainless steel knife to prevent the flesh from turning black. Most people prefer to peel eggplants, as the skin can sometimes be bitter.

Salting eggplant pulls moisture out and keeps it from absorbing large amounts of oil. Cut into rounds, then sprinkle with ½ teaspoon salt per pound of eggplant. Set in a colander for about 30 minutes, rinse, gently squeeze, and pat dry with a towel.

Use in spaghetti sauce or ratatouille or make eggplant Parmesan.

PEPPERS

HEALTH BENEFITS Sweet peppers and hot or chili peppers are related but are significantly different. Both kinds of peppers are good sources of the antioxidant vitamins A and C, but red peppers are simply bursting with these nutrients. Sweet and hot peppers are also chock-full of monoterpenes and polyphenols, warriors against cancer. The white ribs of sweet peppers are rich in bioflavonoids, potent protectors of blood vessels.

Capsaicin, concentrated in the white membranes and seeds of chili peppers, is responsible for hot peppers' heat. It may offer protection against heart attacks and strokes by improving circulation. Capsaicin is a good anti-inflammatory and has decongestant properties, too. It prompts cells in air passages to make more fluids, thinning out congestion and washing away irritants. Similar reactions occur in your nose and eyes when eating spicy, hot food.

Capsaicin's antibacterial properties help fight stomach ulcers caused by *H. pylori* bacteria when taken in small amounts—at most 1–2 peppers per day. Rather than aggravating ulcers, hot peppers help heal them by improving blood flow. Drink ¼ teaspoon cayenne pepper stirred into 1 cup of hot water per day to help ulcers. Higher intakes (4 or more peppers a day) are associated with an increased risk of stomach cancer in some studies. Discontinue if it causes pain or burning.

Capsaicin provides pain relief when taken internally or applied topically. Powdered cayenne pepper made into a poultice can stop wounds from bleeding. Some people will experience burning from a capsaicin poultice. Skin salves with capsaicin treat shingles, itchy psoriasis, and postsurgical pain. The capsaicin in salve is absorbed and provides relief for arthritis and rheumatism. Some naturopathic physicians recommend 25 mg of cayenne pepper taken twice daily to avert migraines.

STORAGE Green peppers can stay firm for a week in a plastic bag in the refrigerator crisper drawer. Non-green peppers are ripe and therefore will go soft after three or four days. Hot peppers do best refrigerated in a perforated paper bag.

PREPARATION AND SERVING TIPS Wash peppers just before using. Trim away the stem and pull out the seeds, but leave the white membrane. Use plastic bags on your hands if handling hot peppers. Wash hands and all utensils with soap after handling peppers to prevent spreading the burning oils.

Bell peppers are delicious raw. Diced, they add delightful crunch and color to sandwich spreads. If you cook them, do so only lightly.

Hot peppers are a great way to add seasoning to just about any food. Too much of them can burn your mouth, in which case drink milk. A protein in milk, called casein, washes away capsaicin, whereas water merely spreads it around.

TOMATOES

HEALTH BENEFITS The tomato's recent claim to fame is its wealth of lycopene, the red carotenoid more potent than the antioxidant beta-carotene. Lycopene appears to be an excellent soldier in the war on prostate cancer. It also protects women from developing precancerous cells of the cervix. People who eat tomato products often have less stomach and lung cancer than those who don't. Lycopene is best absorbed when teamed up with a little bit of oil, preferably a healthy oil such as olive or flax.

STORAGE Store at room temperature for best flavor.

PREPARATION AND SERVING TIPS Alone or in salads, homegrown tomatoes can't be beat.

Chopped tomatoes add flavor and color to just about any dish.

TYPE OF PLANTS Eggplant, peppers, and tomatoes are all tender plants. They are grown as annuals. They need warm temperatures and do not tolerate frost.

WHERE TO GROW These warm-weather nightshades need a long growing season, full sun, and rich soil.

HOW TO GROW Set transplants out about one week after the last frost date, preferably when it's cloudy, or else use newspaper tents to shade them for a day.

Keep well watered and avoid excessive amounts of nitrogen or the plant will produce foliage instead of fruit. Heat above 85–90°F will also discourage production. Mulching will help keep soil temperatures cooler if necessary.

Tomatoes need staking or caging, as they are large plants;

this keeps fruits from rotting on the ground.

HARVEST Pick eggplants before they reach 6 inches in diameter or they may be bitter.

Sweet peppers are typically harvested green. If you want yellow, red, or purple peppers, leave them on the vine. Leaving them will also significantly increase their vitamin A content and somewhat increase their vitamin C content. Don't pull peppers off the vine, or you may uproot the entire plant; instead, cut them from the vine.

Ripe tomatoes will feel firm but not hard. Color depends on variety.

POTATOES

HEALTH BENEFITS One potato has more potassium than half a banana. It is high in vitamin C and is a reasonable source of iron and copper. A potato a day is good for controlling blood pressure and promoting heart health. You'll get the most nutrients and fiber if you also eat the skin.

TYPE OF PLANT Potatoes are underground tubers.

WHERE TO GROW Most potatoes cannot tolerate frost but need a cool climate. Plant in full sun with well-drained soil.

HOW TO GROW Plant whole potatoes or pieces with eyes. Do not use supermarket potatoes, unless they are organic, as they are treated to inhibit sprouting.

Keep plants mulched to protect potatoes from sunburn. Potatoes exposed to light turn green and produce solanine, which is toxic.

HARVESTING For new potatoes, dig up potatoes when the plant blooms. For mature potatoes, dig up with a spading fork two weeks after the plants have died.

STORAGE Store potatoes in a place that is dry, cool, dark, and ventilated. Do not refrigerate or store with onions.

PREPARATION AND SERVING TIPS Scrub potatoes with a brush when ready to cook. If the potato is slightly green, cut away ⅛ inch below the skin to avoid the solanine, a toxic alkaloid.

Baked potatoes topped with steamed vegetables and salsa can make a simple meal. Use cubed potatoes in soups and casseroles. Oven-fry sliced potatoes with a teaspoon of oil and fresh herbs.

PARSLEY

PARSLEY OFFERS a cornucopia of disease-fighting vitamins and healing substances, especially when compared to the lettuces. More nutrient dense than most greens, parsley tops the chart in vitamins A and C and the minerals calcium and iron.

HEALTH BENEFITS Three ounces, or about ten sprigs, of parsley contain more folate than an orange, nearly a day's amount of vitamin C, and more vitamin A in the form of beta-carotene than an apricot. Parsley is a storehouse of minerals, too, with as much calcium as a serving of dark, leafy greens. It's also a good plant source of iron—it contains more iron than most. Parsley is packed full of potassium, too, which helps regulate heartbeat and blood pressure.

Parsley is brimming with strong antioxidants such as lutein, monoterpenes, and polyphenols, which help prevent cancerous cell changes. Polyphenols are natural chemicals in the plant that stop cancerous nitrosamines from forming in the digestive tract.

Parsley is also known for its diuretic properties. Several of the substances in parsley and its seeds are used to treat bladder infections and kidney problems, although human studies have not yet been done to confirm this. Other compounds may reduce inflammation and increase circulation.

TYPE OF PLANT Parsley is a small biennial plant, usually grown as an annual. It is available in three main varieties:

ruffled, Italian, and Hamburg. Ruffled is the most common type in this country, with curly leaves and mild flavor. Italian parsley has flat leaves, has a stronger flavor, and is best used as an herb. Hamburg parsley has roots that taste like celery, a close relative.

WHERE TO GROW Parsley likes full sun but will tolerate partial shade and light frosts. It prefers moist, rich soil. Parsley makes an ideal indoor plant. Set it in a cool room, where it can get about 6 hours of sun per day.

HOW TO GROW Parsley germinates very slowly. Soak seeds for 24 hours before planting and start indoors. It's usually easier to start parsley with transplants. Set out transplants when soil is warm. If your parsley survives a mild winter, it will quickly go to seed in the spring and reseed, or you will need to plant new parsley.

HARVESTING Snip sprigs as needed, leaving enough foliage in the center for the plant to continue growing. Harvest while leaves are small for best flavor and tenderness.

STORAGE Keep in the refrigerator crisper in a plastic bag. Rather than drying extra parsley, freeze it. Dried parsley is rather tasteless. Frozen parsley will be flavorful and sweeter. Wash sprigs thoroughly, air dry, and freeze in a single layer on a cookie sheet; then store in freezer bags.

PREPARATION AND SERVING TIPS Cut off most of the parsley stems and use them in soups, then wash by swishing the leaves in a bowl of water. Remove parsley, run clean water, and repeat until there is no more sand collecting in the bowl. Pat the parsley dry and use as a seasoning, garnish, or main ingredient. Be bold with parsley! Use an entire bunch at a time. Coarsely chopped parsley makes a good addition to any type of lettuce or cabbage salad and boosts the healing properties of the salad. If using it in soups, sauces, or stews, add it near the end of cooking time

PARSNIPS

PARSNIPS ARE HIGH in folate and potassium. Unlike their carrot cousins, parsnips lack beta-carotene; however, they do contain numerous anticancer compounds still being investigated.

HEALTH BENEFITS Parsnips offer a wealth of fiber. A ½ cup serving of cooked parsnips contributes 10–15 percent of the average person's daily fiber needs. Parsnips are abundant in soluble fiber, the type that helps lower cholesterol and keep blood sugar on an even keel. They are also rich in insoluble fiber, the kind that protects against colon cancer. This type of fiber pushes food residue through the colon quickly, sweeping away harmful substances as it goes. This prevents potential cancer-causing compounds from lingering around the cells of the colon wall, where they could potentially start serious trouble.

TYPE OF PLANT Parsnips are root vegetables grown as annuals. They look like whitish–tan-colored carrots and have celerylike leaves.

WHERE TO GROW This vegetable prefers a cool climate and will tolerate freezing temperatures. Parsnips like full sun but will still produce in partial shade. They need loose soil free of rocks and lumps for proper root development.

HOW TO GROW Plant seeds directly into the garden several weeks before the last frost date. Thin seedlings by cutting them off rather than pulling them so as not to disturb the neighbor's roots. Water amply until maturity, then decrease watering to avoid developing cracks in the roots.

HARVESTING The longer parsnips stay in the ground, the sweeter they will taste. The extra time plus a frost allows the starch to turn into sugar.

Moisten the soil, then pull up small to medium-size parsnips.

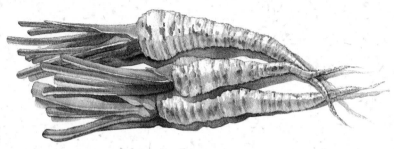

Don't let them get large, or they will be tough and fibrous.

STORAGE Clip off any attached greens before refrigerating to prevent draining moisture from the parsnips. Put them into a loosely closed plastic bag in the crisper drawer of the refrigerator. They will keep for a couple of weeks.

PREPARATION AND SERVING TIPS
Scrub parsnips well with a vegetable brush. Trim both ends. As with carrots, cut ½ inch off the top to avoid garden chemical residues.

Parsnips are not usually eaten raw. Scrape or peel a thin layer of skin before or after cooking. If you do it after, they'll retain more nutrients and be sweeter.

Because of their shape, whole parsnips don't cook evenly.

Make two lengthwise slices through the thick end to help even out the cooking times. Alternatively, cut parsnips in half crosswise and cook the thick ends first, adding the thin portion halfway through cooking. Steaming takes about 20 to 30 minutes. To speed cooking, cut them into rounds and steam for 10 minutes or until tender when pierced with a fork.

Serve diced parsnips and carrots mixed together for a pretty fall dish. They can also substitute for potatoes; just purée them with a little bit of olive oil. To bring out their sweetness, add ginger, dill weed, chervil, or nutmeg.

Parsnips are great in soups and stews. They add flavor to the stock, or they can be puréed and used as a thickener.

PLUMS

THERE ARE HUNDREDS of kinds of plums, and they all have healing properties. What a delicious way to protect blood vessels, fight free radicals, and help prevent cancer. Eat several of them and you'll have received useful amounts of vitamins A and C, potassium, and fiber.

HEALTH BENEFITS Plums contain flavonoids, some of the phytochemicals that give plants their colors and help people stay cancer-free because of their antioxidant activities. Some of these substances protect blood vessels from damage that triggers plaque buildup and protect the tiniest capillaries from bursting or bruising.

Potassium is a team player when it comes to preventing heart problems. Fiber in the plums' colorful peels promotes a healthy colon, while the soluble fiber in the flesh helps normalize blood cholesterol and blood sugar levels.

Plums contain sorbitol, a natural sugar. Large amounts can have mildly laxative effects. Some people are unable to completely digest sorbitol, experiencing gas, abdominal cramps, and diarrhea. However, eating a few plums is not a problem for most people.

TYPE OF PLANT Plums are deciduous, broadly spreading trees that reach about 30 feet in height. Fruit is round or oval shaped; green, yellow, red, or purple in color; and about two to three inches in length. Some are grown not just to be eaten fresh, but to be dried into prunes. Japanese and European are the two main varieties. Several common plums good for eating include Santa Rosa, Friar, Red Beauty, El Dorado, Greengage, and Kelsey.

WHERE TO GROW Plum trees grow in most climates throughout North America as long as they get full sun and have well-drained soil.

HOW TO GROW This is one plant you don't need a green thumb to be able to grow. Generally speaking, plums don't mind poor soil conditions and can even be neglected without harm.

HARVESTING Harvest ripe plums when they yield to gentle pressure. Let them just start to soften. The taste test is probably the best way to determine ripeness; fruit should be soft, juicy, and sweet. Plums are often covered with a powdery "bloom," which gives them a dusty appearance. This bloom is their protective coat.

STORAGE As long as plums are not picked when hard, they will continue to ripen. However, they won't get sweeter, just softer. To ripen plums, place them in a loosely closed paper bag at room temperature. Check frequently so they won't get shriveled or moldy. When they are slightly soft, refrigerate or eat them.

PREPARATION AND SERVING TIPS Wash plums right before you're ready to use them to enable the protective bloom to stay on the fruit. Like most fruits, they taste best at room temperature or just slightly cooler.

Many Japanese plums are best eaten fresh, whereas most European varieties are best cooked in jams or preserves, canned, or stewed.

A traditional way to serve plums is in a compote, a combination of warm, stewed, sweetened fruits. Purée peeled plums to serve with poultry or game. Plum sauce can be mixed into yogurt or served over ice milk.

SALAD GREENS

SALAD GREENS perk up the taste, texture, and healing benefits of your daily salad. The more color there is, the more nutrients are packed into the leaves. Dark green or red leaves are rich in antioxidants, vitamin C, iron, calcium, and folate.

HEALTH BENEFITS Leaf lettuces contain many more vitamins, minerals, and phytochemicals than iceberg, or crisphead, lettuce. Although iceberg is most commonly used for salads, it contains only negligible amounts of nutrients. Instead, it would be wise to allot garden space to greens that give a boost to your body. Romaine, for instance, has about six times more vitamin C and about ten times more beta-carotene than iceberg. Romaine also has the cancer-fighting carotenoids lutein and zeaxanthin. All these antioxidants appear to protect against heart disease, strokes, and cataracts. Nutritionally speaking, other leaf lettuces lie between iceberg and romaine. So use romaine or leaf lettuces as a base for your salad. Then add some of the other greens mentioned below to jazz up the nutrient content of your salad.

Wonderfully flavorful greens such as raddichio, arugula, watercress, chicory, cilantro, and escarole add new tastes, textures, and more healing nutrients to your salads. Here are some of the more common varieties of these previously less-than-common salad greens:

Arugula: Once a hard-to-find green, bold-flavored arugula is becoming more popular. Its flavor is somewhat peppery and nutty at the same time. It tastes best when grown in cool weather. As leaves get larger, their flavor becomes more mustardlike. Use in small quantities with other greens. Arugula is rich in vitamin A as beta-carotene and vitamin C. Arugula is also called rocket or roquette.

Chicory: This curly-leaved dark green is sometimes mistakenly called curly endive. However, it does produce the light-colored shoots called Belgian endive. The dark-green leaves have a bitter taste, but they work well in salads that have strongly seasoned dressings.

Bitter greens aid digestion. If you have trouble with indigestion, include some bitter greens in each salad. (Roasted chicory comes from the roasted ground roots and is used as a coffee substitute.)

Escarole: A close cousin to chicory, escarole is actually a type of endive. It has broad,

slightly curved green leaves and has a milder flavor than Belgian endive. Its rich green color means it's full of nutrients.

Lamb's Lettuce: This is a delicate green that grows in cool weather. Its tender leaves have a sweet, mild flavor.

Raddichio: Though it looks something like a miniature head of red cabbage, this salad green is actually a member of the varied chicory family, although it is less bitter. Its bitterness will mellow if grown in cool weather. Full of carotenes, raddichio will provide your body with an ample supply of antioxidants. There are two categories of raddichio, choggia and treviso, both of which contain several varieties.

Watercress: This delicate green is absolutely bursting with nutrients. It even outranks romaine lettuce and is right up there with cooking greens like kale and chard. Extremely rich in minerals, coarsely chopped watercress will jump-start any salad with its mildly tangy flavor.

Typically, you can count on salad greens to provide you with nutrients such as vitamin C and A that may boost immunity; folate, which protects against birth defects and heart disease; and potassium, which promotes heart health. In addition, the more colorful greens contribute a wide array of phytochemicals that demolish cell-damaging free radicals, thus helping to prevent mutated DNA, which can start cancerous growths. These protective substances help ward off strokes and heart disease, too. Most salad greens have at least a little bit of fiber, which helps keep the colon tuned up and disease free.

TYPE OF PLANT Lettuces and salad greens are generally hardy, fast-growing annuals. Some varieties can form heads, while others form loose leaves.

WHERE TO GROW These greens prefer a cool climate. If you live in a warm climate, accommodate these plants by growing them in spring, fall, and even winter. Iceberg, or crisphead, lettuce does not grow well in the home garden. Leaf lettuces are much succesful.

Salad greens need well-worked soil that can retain moisture but drains well.

HOW TO GROW Plant seeds directly into the garden four to six weeks before the date of the last frost. If you live in a hot area, start seeds indoors two months or more before the last frost date, and transplant as soon as possible to allow the plants to mature before hot weather sets in. Starting about midsummer, sow succession crops for fall harvesting. Hot weather can make plants bolt, which means they produce reproductive flowers and seed rather than the intended product.

When true leaves appear on seedlings, thin leaf lettuces to 8 inches apart and head lettuces to about 12 inches apart. Crowding will prevent head lettuces from forming properly and can trigger bolting.

Salad greens need an ample supply of water, so be careful not to let the plants dry out.

Watercress needs to grow in flowing water, if you have a stream on your property. Otherwise, put seeds in small pots of well-limed soil and sit in pans of water about 6 inches deep. Change water daily.

HARVESTING Pick the outer leaves as the greens grow, letting the inner leaves continue to develop. Alternatively, cut the entire plant off at ground level. Harvest in the morning or when weather is cool, otherwise leaves may be limp. Don't harvest watercress from the wild, as it looks like similar poisonous plants and it can be contaminated with *Giardia lamblia*.

STORAGE Store lettuce and salad greens unwashed in the refrigerator crisper drawer in plastic bags. Discard any leaves that are wilted, have brown edges, or are slimy.

PREPARATION AND SERVING TIPS
Wash salad greens thoroughly before using, making sure to remove all sand. Cut off the base and swish in a bowl or sink of water. If greens are limp, an ice water bath can revive them.

Several of these salad greens can also be grilled, sautéed, or baked as cooking greens. Add a sturdy lettuce to pasta by combining with sautéed garlic and black beans, cooking just enough to wilt. Toss with hot pasta and grated Parmesan cheese. In general, the stronger and more bitter the salad green, the stronger the dressing needs to be. Watercress can be used to make a light sauce for fish or a delicious base for soup.

SEEDS

SEEDS ARE AMONG the best plant sources of iron and zinc and provide more fiber per ounce than nuts. They are also good sources of protein, essential amino acids, iron, and vitamin E.

PUMPKIN SEEDS

HEALTH BENEFITS Pumpkin seeds are a well-known folk remedy for maintaining a healthy prostate and expelling intestinal parasites. They're packed full of nutrients that provide support for and will even shrink an enlarged prostate gland. Researchers have found that zinc and the amino acids alanine, glycine, and glutamic acid reduce many of the urinary problems associated with the enlarged gland. About ½ cup pumpkin seeds a day will keep the prostate from enlarging and help keep an already enlarged prostate from worsening.

Tryptophan is another amino acid that's plentiful in pumpkin seeds. Tryptophan is a natural antidepressant but is available in supplement form by prescription only. Physicians have found that eating large quantities of pumpkin seeds supplied enough tryptophan to coax the brain into making more serotonin, a mood-regulating chemical in the brain. Elevated serotonin levels foster a feeling of well-being.

SUNFLOWER SEEDS

HEALTH BENEFITS With good levels of B vitamins thiamin, niacin, and B_6, sunflower seeds provide the nutrients your body needs to process food into energy and to make protein. About 3 ounces provide more than the day's requirement for thiamin, one-third the amount of niacin you need in a day, and about one-half the required amount of B_6.

TYPE OF PLANT Pumpkins and sunflowers are annuals. Sunflowers range from 1–15 feet in height. The large varieties are the best at producing seeds.

WHERE TO GROW These plants will grow just about anywhere in the United States. Pumpkins need a long growing season and are sensitive to frost. Neither plant requires much fertilizer. Pumpkins like well-drained soil, whereas sunflowers do not. Both need full sun. Sunflowers should be grown at the back or north side of the garden, where they won't shade other plants.

HOW TO GROW Plant pumpkins from seeds in hills about 6 feet apart after danger of frost has past. Put several seeds in each hill and thin to one plant. Pumpkins need ample amounts of water to encourage steady growth.

Seed sunflowers directly into the garden after the last frost. Tall sunflowers may need to be staked for support. As sunflower seeds develop, tie netting around the heads to prevent birds from getting them before you do.

HARVESTING Leave pumpkins on the vine as long as possible before the first frost. Leave 1 or 2 inches of stem when harvesting pumpkins. Cut off the sunflower heads with enough stem remaining to hang upside down. Allow the seeds to dry, then remove them from the head.

STORAGE Because of their high fat content, seeds are vulnerable to rancidity. Once harvested, store in the refrigerator, where they'll keep for several months.

PREPARATION AND SERVING TIPS A great way to benefit from seeds' nutritional warehouse without getting too much fat is to mix them in with cereals or dried fruit.

SPINACH

SPINACH'S BEAUTIFUL deep green color is a tip-off that it contains plenty of beta-carotene; those orange and red carotene pigments are hiding beneath the dark green chlorophyll. Spinach is also an excellent source of vitamin C, folate, and iron.

HEALTH BENEFITS Spinach is a cornucopia of cancer fighters. For example, it has triple the amount of lutein and four times the amount of beta-carotene as broccoli. These antioxidants not only help prevent cancer, heart disease, and cataracts, but also boost the immune system. One study found that eating spinach more than twice a week was corelated with reduced risk of breast cancer. This vegetable contains a lot of folate, too. McGill University researchers found that folate improves serotonin levels in the brain, inducing a calm feeling of well-being. A daily dose of cooked spinach—¾ of a cup—alleviated depression in study participants.

Spinach has the mineral manganese, too, which works with other minerals to strengthen bones. Although spinach is rich in calcium, the body is not able to absorb much of it. That's because spinach contains a compound called oxalic acid that binds with calcium, making it unavailable to the body. People who are prone to developing the most common type of kidney stones will want to limit their intake of spinach and rhubarb because the oxalic acid in these foods can promote the formation of stones.

TYPE OF PLANT Spinach is a hardy annual that comes in two basic varieties: curly leafed or smooth. It is related to beets and chard. So-called New Zealand spinach is not really spinach at all, but a plant from a different family. However, it is nutritionally similar to true spinach but doesn't contain oxalic acid.

WHERE TO GROW Spinach thrives in cold climates and can grow throughout winter in warm climates. Plant in an area that has rich, well-drained soil. In cool climates it grows best in spring and fall. It will tolerate partial shade.

HOW TO GROW Plant seed clusters about one month before the last frost. Each seed cluster will produce several seedlings, which need to be thinned. Keep soil moist. Use mulch to retain moisture and reduce the amount of soil that gets onto the leaves.

HARVESTING Snip off outside leaves occasionally, choosing those that are crisp and dark green. The entire plant can also be pulled up.

STORAGE Refrigerate spinach greens in a plastic bag. Leaves should keep for three to four days. Wash right before you're ready to prepare the greens. Discard limp or yellowing leaves. If you wash before storing, the leaves will deteriorate rapidly.

PREPARATION AND SERVING TIPS Wash spinach leaves in a sink or bowl of cool water right before preparing them. Discard water and repeat the rinsing process two or three times until all sand is gone.

Sweet vinaigrette dressings complement spinach's slightly bitter flavor. For classic spinach salad, omit the usual bacon and egg yolks and try mushrooms and garbanzo beans instead.

To cook spinach, simmer it in very little water for a short period of time, just until wilted and tender. Top it off with lemon juice, seasoned vinegar, sautéed garlic, or a dash of nutmeg.

SQUASH

THE SQUASH FAMILY can be divided into two main categories: summer and winter. The more colorful flesh of the winter squash tends to be richer in alpha- and beta-carotene and several B vitamins.

HEALTH BENEFITS Winter squashes have a plentiful supply of alpha- and beta-carotene. These carotenes can both be turned into vitamin A in the body, although beta-carotene is more efficiently handled. All this vitamin A keeps the eyes healthy and aids night vision. Beta-carotene has been found to reduce the incidence of strokes. And if a stroke does occur, high beta-carotene levels in the bloodstream enhance recovery. Carotenes may also slow the rate at which cancerous cells multiply and improve the communication systems between healthy cells. As yet, research has not shown if eating squash brings the same benefit shown in studies using isolated carotenes.

The large amount of potassium in winter or summer squashes may help regulate your heartbeat and normalize your blood pressure. Reasonable amounts of calcium and fiber are also found behind the colorful skins, so don't peel them until after they've been cooked; then carefully try to retain as much flesh as possible.

TYPE OF PLANT All squashes are very tender annuals with weak stems. Summer squashes grow bushlike, producing fruits with edible skin, flesh, and seeds. Winter squashes grow on a vine, producing fruits with edible flesh, tough skins that are largely inedible, and seeds that need to be shelled before eating.

WHERE TO GROW Squashes need to be grown in warm, rich soil with good drainage. They do not tolerate frost and don't like cold weather.

HOW TO GROW Plant 3 or 4 seeds in hills about three weeks after the date of the last frost. If starting with transplants, make sure the containers are plantable so as not to disturb the roots. Thin to the strongest 2 or 3 plants. Squash requires a lot of water, so keep the soil moist. If leaves are wilted in the morning, water immediately. Fertilize frequently.

HARVESTING Summer squashes are best harvested when young and small for best flavor and texture. Left on the bush, they will discourage further production. Long squashes should not get larger than 6 to 8 inches, while round squash should be 4 to 6 inches in diameter.

Winter squashes need to be left on the vine until the skin is very hard. Cut or break from the stem before the first frost, then cure in a warm, dark place for about 10 days.

STORAGE Summer squash keep for a few days in the crisper of the refrigerator. Do not wash before storing. If muddy, winter squash can be washed, then dried and stored in a cool, dry, dark place. Winter squash will keep for up to six months.

PREPARATION AND SERVING TIPS Summer squash is easily sliced or grated and can be served raw in salads. The entire squash, seeds and all, can also be cooked. Steam lightly and top with fresh chopped herbs. Or panfry with garlic in a nonstick pan coated with cooking spray.

The skin of winter squash is very tough. Use a large, sharp knife and be careful! After removing the seeds, winter squash can be baked, steamed, or added to soups. Try sweet herbs such as allspice, cinnamon, cloves, and nutmeg to bring out flavor.

SWEET POTATOES

SWEET POTATOES ARE among the unsung heroes of healthy eating. Nutrient-packed with only a few calories, sweet potatoes support immune function, eyesight, heart health, and cancer protection.

HEALTH BENEFITS Teeming with beta-carotene, sweet potatoes outrank carrots by far in this healthful nutrient. This benefi-cial antioxidant wages a continuous battle against free radicals and the diseases they trigger, including cancer. In a study at Harvard University, people who ate ¾ cup cooked sweet potatoes, carrots, or spinach every day (all foods high in beta-carotene) had a 40 percent lower risk of experiencing a stroke. Researchers theorized that this nutrient protects blood choles-terol from undergoing damage from oxygen molecules. Dam-aged cholesterol begins the artery-clogging process. Other studies show that the more beta-carotene and vitamin A stroke patients have in their bloodstream, the less likely they are to die from the stroke and the more likely they are to make a full recovery.

All this beta-carotene also promotes healthy eyes and vision, since much of it gets turned into vitamin A as the body needs it. This wonder nutrient also works with certain white blood cells, tuning up your immune system to fight off colds, flu, and other illnesses.

Sweet potatoes rank right up with bananas as a source of potassium, the heart-friendly nutrient. These colorful roots are a surprisingly good source of vitamin C.

TYPE OF PLANT Sweet potatoes come in two varieties: dry and moist. The moist ones are often called yams, but this is a misnomer. True yams grow in tropical areas. Sweet potatoes are very tender perennials grown as annuals. Their fleshy roots range from creamy-yellow (dry) to deep red-orange (moist) in color.

WHERE TO GROW Sweet potatoes need a moist climate with a long growing season. They cannot tolerate frost. Plant in mounded ridges in an area with loose soil that is not particularly rich.

HOW TO GROW Start sweet potatoes from rooted sprouts taken from a mature root. To grow sprouts, put sweet potatoes in a cold frame and cover with two inches of light soil. Keep warm. Add more soil when shoots appear. The shoots will develop roots, which can be planted. Put out about one month after the date of the last frost. Sweet potatoes need a steady supply of water until about three weeks before harvesting.

HARVESTING Dig up potatoes with a spade fork before the first frost. The roots are easily damaged in cold soil.

STORAGE Sweet potatoes may look hardy, but they are actually fragile and spoil easily. Surface cuts and bruises spread quickly. Store in a cool, dark place but do not refrigerate. If potatoes develop a white stringy "beard," they are overmature and probably tough and stringy.

PREPARATION AND SERVING TIPS When cooked, the yellow (dry) variety resembles a baked potato in texture. In fact, the dry variety is an excellent substitute for white potatoes. The orange variety, much sweeter and moister, is the typical Thanksgiving dish. The moist variety also works well mashed, in a soufflé, or in traditional Southern sweet-potato pie. Cook sweet potatoes with their skins on to preserve nutrients and keep in the natural sugar.

THIS GENTLY FLAVORED VEGETABLE is chock-full of beta-carotene and its relatives lutein and zeaxanthin, all potent disease fighters and immune boosters. The minerals potassium and magnesium, along with vitamin C, also hide in these beautifully colored, crinkled leaves.

HEALTH BENEFITS Chard's carotenoids are strong protectors against cancer, heart disease, strokes, cataracts, and maybe even aging. Studies have not addressed whether eating chard confers these same protective benefits. Some researchers believe that antioxidants such as these prevent wear and tear on cells, thus reducing the number of times they need to reproduce within a person's lifetime and possibly slowing down the aging process. Chard also contains reasonable amounts of vitamin C, another antioxidant.

Potassium provides a head start against heart problems, and chard has an abundance of it. You need plenty of this mineral if you take diuretics that don't "spare potassium," meaning they make your body lose its potassium reserves. If you take diuretics, check with your doctor to see whether you should be on the lookout for extra potassium.

Even though chard is full of calcium and iron, like spinach, it's not very absorbable. Chard, too, is rich in oxalic acid, which binds these minerals.

Some people shy away from chard, having heard that it is high in sodium. One-half cup cooked chard does contain 158 mg of sodium, but this is just a fraction of the daily maximum recommended of 2400 mg. (However, our bodies only need 200 mg per day.) Processed foods such as crackers, chips, canned soups, and lunchmeats have many times more sodium than chard, and often without the plethora of healing nutrients.

TYPE OF PLANT Swiss chard is grown as an annual. It is closely related to beets. Also known just as chard, this plant has large, dark green leaves. The stalks can be either red or white, with red varieties having a stronger flavor.

WHERE TO PLANT Chard likes a cool climate with rich, well-drained soil. It dislikes acidic conditions.

HOW TO PLANT Plant seed clusters in rows directly into the garden about one week before the last frost date. Thin appropriately. Chard needs ample water so the leaves will grow steadily; keep the soil moist.

HARVESTING Begin harvesting when leaves are about 3 inches long. Choose small, tender, green ones, taking a few at a time to keep the plant producing all season. Alternatively, cut all leaves down to about 3 inches and let the plant regrow. Avoid leaves that are yellow.

STORAGE Store unwashed, dry leaves in a plastic bag in the refrigerator. Chard will keep for three or four days.

PREPARATION AND SERVING TIPS When ready to prepare, rinse chard thoroughly to remove all dirt from leaf crevices. Most varieties in this country have good-tasting leaves, whereas varieties in other parts of the world have been developed to have tender, good-tasting stalks as well. Trim the stalk out of the leaf if desired; they take longer to cook than the leaves. Chard goes well in soups and mixed dishes such as casseroles or quiches. Or steam it lightly and toss with a little sautéed onion and garlic. To avoid discoloration, do not prepare it in an iron pot. Eaten raw, chard makes an excellent substitute for spinach.

HERB PROFILES

GELATINLIKE SUBSTANCES inside aloe leaves are well-known for their ability to soothe and heal skin. Applied topically, it diminishes pain and helps heal minor open wounds. Taken internally, extracts of aloe may boost the body's ability to battle cancer and other diseases.

HEALING PROPERTIES

Researchers find that aloe excels when it comes to most skin problems, including burns, abrasions, reactions to poison oak and ivy, dandruff, eczema, frostbite, ringworm, and even gum disease. It is also used for radiation burns, although a recent clinical study could not confirm a benefit. A compound in aloe called chrysophanic acid limits the amount of tissue-damaging substances the body makes when reacting to an injury. It also contains allantoin, which promotes healthy tissue growth. Thus, aloe speeds up wound healing. It also stimulates the immune system and can help prevent wound infection. Aloe has shown direct antibacterial activity in test tubes. Keep an aloe plant on a windowsill to use undiluted sap for instant relief. Creams and lotions that contain aloe are also good to keep on hand, although they may not contain enough aloe to be helpful. At least one study showed that an aloe-rich cream helps psoriasis.

Another substance found in aloe's gel, acemannan, may be effective in treating people with cancer and diseases related to a lack of white blood cells. Veterinarians have been using aloe extracts to treat animals with cancer and leukemia. Scientists theorize that acemannan encourages the body to make more white blood cells—especially the type that eliminate mutated cancer-causing cells and fight invaders like bacteria and viruses.

Aloe's bitter latex is a cathartic laxative, so it needs to be used with care. It can exacerbate diarrhea, sometimes enough to be quite a problem.

Studies have shown that taking 1 teaspoon of aloe gel twice a day can be a helpful therapy for people with diabetes.

TYPE OF PLANT
There are more than 300 varieties of this plant, which is perennial in areas devoid of frost. Aloe vera is the most common; it is native to warm, tropical climates. It resembles cactus, with long, spiny, pointed leaves that are thick, succulent, and full of mucilaginous sap. It can grow 1–3 feet in diameter and several feet tall. It will produce an orange-red flower stalk in two to three years.

HOW TO GROW Aloe does not tolerate frosts; it needs warm weather year-round. It only requires average soil, as long as it is well-drained. Aloe likes filtered sun and shade. It does not need much water and tolerates drought well.

Seeds can take months to germinate. It is easier to start plants from the offshoots of established plants. Remove the offshoot and plant in loose soil. Aloe grows very well indoors in a warm room with partial sun. All indoor plants need adequate circulation. If windows are closed, keep a fan in the room, but do not aim it at the plants. Aloe plants live for many years.

HARVESTING Cut off the outermost leaves as you need them; new ones grow from the center. If you break off just a portion of a leaf to use, the leaf will mend its own cut, saving its special gel for you to use later. It's best to refrigerate the whole leaf or section.

PREPARATION AND DOSAGE Slice a leaf lengthwise to scrape out the healing sap. Mash with a fork. Spread as needed on skin and wounds. Add powdered or liquid vitamin C to preserve extra sap and refrigerate if you're not going to use it all at once.

If taking internally, use only commercially prepared juices to avoid potentially harmful substances.

PRECAUTIONS A yellow layer just beneath the skin of the leaf has strong laxative effects and causes extreme cramping. The substance responsible for this action is removed in commercially prepared aloe juice.

Aloe should not be used on large or infected wounds as it may cause premature wound closure, trapping bacteria and exacerbating the problem. At least one study has documented this possibility.

If you are taking medications including insulin while taking aloe, you must be carefully monitored as there could be a dangerous reduction in blood sugar levels.

ANGELICA

THERE ARE TWO general types of angelica—garden angelica and dong quai, or Chinese angelica—which must be carefully distinguished because they have different properties.

HEALING PROPERTIES Angelica is widely used to stimulate digestion and ease indigestion. It prompts the flow of stomach acid and digestive juices. It soothes the stomach and intestines, alleviating colic and flatulence. It is particularly helpful for decreasing spasms of all kinds, including coughs and intestinal spasms.

This herb is a potent expectorant and cough suppressant. Its healing compounds treat bronchial conditions, colds, and asthma. Given as a hot infusion, angelica induces sweating and helps ease the misery of a cold. It also has mild antibacterial and antifungal properties.

Angelica's diuretic and antimicrobial properties make it useful as part of a protocol for eliminating bladder infections.

In Japan, anti-inflammatory properties have been discovered in a related species of angelica. This makes the herb promising for arthritis relief.

A woman's friend, angelica eases menstrual cramps and normalizes menstrual flow. Its close relative *Angelica sinensis*, also known as Chinese angelica or dong quai, helps alleviate menstrual problems. However, dong quai should be avoided during menstrual bleeding as the herb can cause increased bleeding. This variety is also used to improve liver function in patients with chronic hepatitis or cirrhosis. Preliminary research indicates Chinese angelica may be a cancer fighter, too.

TYPE OF PLANT *Angelica archangelica* is a large biennial herb. Its lush growth spreads up to 3 feet across. Angelica likes moist areas such as marshes, streams, swamps, and meadows. Its foliage resembles that of a parsnip plant. It produces large flower heads made up of clusters of tiny white blossoms and yellow-green seed heads.

HOW TO GROW Angelica's seeds are sensitive to aging. You will have the best luck germinating them if they are less than six months old. Sow seeds in late fall. Angelica can also be started from transplants, but mature plants do not do well if moved.

Choose a cool, moist location with well-drained soil for planting this herb. Angelica likes shade but will tolerate partial sun if necessary.

HARVESTING Do not attempt to harvest angelica from the wild—it closely resembles the deadly poisonous water hemlock. All parts of angelica may be used. Leaves and stems can be harvested anytime. Wait until the plant's first fall or second spring to harvest its roots.

PREPARATION AND DOSAGE Hang stems and leaves to dry or freeze them for later use. Make infusions or tinctures from angelica. Use 1 cup of tea or ¼–½ teaspoon tincture per day.

PRECAUTIONS Because angelica looks like water hemlock, do not harvest it from the wild to avoid accidental poisoning. Children have been poisoned by very tiny amounts.

Pregnant women need to avoid the herb because of its effects on menstrutation.

Angelica contains substances called psoralens that cause some people to develop a rash after being exposed to sunlight. Occasionally it is reported that the leaves are irritating, bringing on dermatitis after they are handled.

THIS PLANT IS USED by herbalists for external treatment of wounds and sore muscles and by homeopathic physicians for stimulating circulation and reducing fevers.

HEALING PROPERTIES Arnica contains several healing phyto-chemicals, including helenalin and arnicin. These substances have pain-relieving, anti-inflammatory, and antiseptic properties. In Germany and throughout Europe, arnica is used in commercial drug formulas that are applied topically for pain relief. Used in salve or liniment form, arnica works wonders on stiff, sore muscles. It penetrates easily, reduces inflammation, and eases pain. The bright yellow flowers of this herb also help heal sprains and bruises. Traditionally, Native Americans used arnica for these same purposes.

In animal studies, arnica increased immune function by stimulating the action of certain white blood cells that attack and destroy harmful bacteria. It was particularly effective against salmonella.

Arnica is an important herb in homeopathy. This branch of natural medicine embraces the philosophy that "like cures like," which means that a small dose of a substance can cure the symptoms of an illness that it would cause if given in large doses. It's a principle similar to that of vaccinations or allergy shots. To prepare a homeopathic arnica remedy, small amounts of the herb are repeatedly diluted in water. Drops of this remedy are then ingested for such purposes as reabsorption of internal bleeding, stimulation of heart and circulation, and fever reduction. Homeopathic remedies can be purchased at natural food stores; the dilutions cannot be prepared at home.

TYPE OF PLANT Arnica is a perennial, resembling a yellow daisy, but is very hard to identify except for the experienced botanist. The plant is slender, reaching 1–2 feet in height. It has hairy stems that produce 1–3 flower stalks during the summer months. Its leaves are slightly hairy on the topside.

HOW TO GROW This wildflower typically lives in mountainous areas. If you give it plenty of sun and sandy, dry soil with humus, it will grow in your healing garden. Start arnica with seeds, divisions, or cuttings taken in the spring.

HARVESTING Harvest the flowers in midsummer or whenever they reach their peak. They are the most potent part of the plant and the one most often used; however, leaves are occasionally harvested, too.

PREPARATION AND DOSAGE For best results, use this herb fresh.

Flowers can be preserved in alcohol to make liniment.

Use arnica oil in tinctures, salves, and ointments. Make your own oil by heating 1 ounce of flowers in 10 ounces of vegetable oil for several hours on low heat. Strain and cool before using.

A compress made with arnica tea or diluted tincture can be applied to wounds, sprains, and bruises. However, do not apply to open wounds as you may absorb dangerous amounts. It soothes intestinal pain when placed on the abdomen.

PRECAUTIONS Do not take arnica internally except in homeopathic form. This herb is for external use only. If consumed, it can cause dizziness and high blood pressure, irritate the gastrointestinal tract and kidneys, and cause internal hemorrhage and death.

Externally, the helenalin in arnica is reported to occasionally cause dermatitis in some people after repeated use.

THIS PURPLISH-BLUE BERRY contains many of the same healing phytochemicals, vitamins, and minerals as do its berry cousins. Anthocyanidins, the flavonoids that give the berry its color, are powerful antioxidants.

HEALING PROPERTIES Bilberry's tart fruit has constituents in it that are helpful to people with diabetes. Typically, people with diabetes are concerned about damage to small blood vessels from excessive sugar in the blood. Anthocyanidins in the berries protect these small blood vessels, thereby averting eye problems, kidney failure, and poor circulation in the extremities. These benign-looking berries stimulate blood vessels to expand, keep blood platelets from sticking together, prevent clotting, and improve blood circulation. This not only helps avoid typical complications of the disease, but also helps prevent heart disease in everyone.

Anthocyanidins assist blood vessels in other ways, such as improving elasticity to help avoid bruises. If bruises do occur, they heal more quickly when anthocyanidins are plentiful in the bloodstream. These compounds help prevent varicose veins and swelling of the feet and ankles.

Bilberry may be helpful for treating eye conditions such as cataracts, night blindness, and macular degeneration. It is widely used in Europe in prescription medications to improve eyesight. It is prescribed for diabetic retinopathy, a common complication that robs many diabetics of their vision.

This herb's berries have been used for years in various cultures to support the digestive tract. German physicians have also found it to be antiemetic, and it may block the activity of bacterial toxins. The dried berries are also a useful treatment for diarrhea. Researchers in Germany are investigating the use of bilberry leaves to treat rheumatism and gout.

Like their berry cousins, bilberries are powerhouses of vitamin C and A, potassium, and fiber. The potassium maintains heart health. The soluble fiber helps lower blood cholesterol levels and stabilize blood sugar levels. The insoluble and soluble fiber in bilberries keep the colon in optimal health.

TYPE OF PLANT Bilberry is a deciduous shrub. It grows throughout North America, typically in wooded areas. It is related to blueberries and huckleberries.

HOW TO GROW Normally a wild bush, new shrubs can be started from cuttings. This herb likes acidic conditions with partially decayed, moist soil. It prefers partial shade. Plant rooted cuttings in spring or fall.

HARVESTING Gather leaves at any time they are green. Harvest berries when they turn deep purple.

PREPARATION AND DOSAGE Bilberry's tart berries can be eaten raw or made into jam or medicinal syrup. Take up to 2 teaspoons of the syrup per day. Berries can also be made into tea or tincture. Use ½–1 teaspoon tincture up to three times per day. If using capsules, take two to six per day.

Bilberries freeze well—place the washed berries on a cookie sheet in a single layer. Once the berries are frozen, scoop them into resealable bags and freeze.

PRECAUTIONS Blood sugar levels must be carefully monitored if you're taking bilberry leaves and insulin. If you start to feel shaky or irritable or get sweaty palms, eat something.

BURDOCK IS FAMOUS for improving digestion and supporting liver function. It is also used to treat skin conditions, especially when they are a result of poor diet, constipation, or stress on the liver. It may also help the liver metabolize hormones, improving conditions associated with hormone imbalances.

HEALING PROPERTIES This herb is considered to be an alterative agent. This means that it improves digestion and absorption while promoting the elimination of wastes. Its bitter root stimulates the production of digestive juices—the acids, enzymes, and bile it takes to break your food apart so nutrients can be absorbed.

By supporting the liver, burdock has far-reaching effects. The liver is responsible for metabolizing, storing, and distributing nutrients. It also produces bile to aid fat digestion and detoxifies harmful substances that pass through it. The liver removes many of the impurities we encounter from modern-day living, such as air pollutants and food additives. If the liver is overworked or not up to par, the toxins it can't remove may cause numerous symptoms, such as headaches, nausea, skin irritations, and even arthritis.

A poultice of burdock leaves effectively speeds the healing of bruises, swelling, and burns. This herb is also used as a diuretic and to induce sweating and relieve constipation.

Several test tube studies suggest it may help fight cancer as well.

TYPE OF PLANT Burdock is a biennial plant that can be grown as an annual. It has many coarse branches and very large leaves. Each branch tip flowers during summer, and it produces seed burrs. The plant reaches about 6 feet in height with a 3-foot spread. It grows wild throughout North America, especially in sunny, damp areas.

HOW TO GROW This herb grows easily from seed or young transplants. Mature plants develop a long taproot and do not like to be moved. Start plants in the spring in an area with moist but well-drained, average soil. Choose a spot that gets full sun, although burdock will tolerate filtered sun.

HARVESTING You can harvest most parts of this plant—roots, leaves, and seeds—but roots are the most commonly used portion. Snip leaves before flowers bloom, and gather seeds after the flowers mature. Dig up roots during the plant's first fall or second spring.

PREPARATION AND DOSAGE Consume burdock root as a vegetable or dry it for tea and medicinal purposes. Limit tea to 2–4 cups per day and tincture to 1 teaspoon three times per day. Taken 15–30 minutes before a meal, burdock root tea improves digestion. It also makes a good coffee substitute.

Burdock can be purchased in Asian markets. In Japanese and macrobiotic cuisine, where this root is a staple, it is called gobo root. Its flavor is fairly strong and might be described as a cross between potatoes and celery. Prepare it fresh, steamed, or sautéed—use it like carrots. You will probably start to notice its effects in about three weeks; use it for two or three months at a time.

PRECAUTIONS Burdock may cause trouble if you have ulcers, irritable bowel syndrome, or excessive stomach acid. However, a qualified practitioner may prescribe it for these conditions under special circumstances. Avoid burdock if you have diarrhea or a flare-up of ulcers or if you experience frequent heartburn.

BUTCHER'S BROOM

THIS PLANT EARNED its name from frequent use by butchers in the 16th–19th centuries to repel undesirable animals and vermin from their shops. Eventually its leaves were gathered into brooms to clean butcher's chopping blocks. We now know that the leaves contain chrysophanic acid, an antimicrobial agent that may reduce harmful bacteria on cutting surfaces.

HEALING PROPERTIES Today the root of butcher's broom is widely used to treat circulatory problems. In Germany, researchers found that it reduced inflammation in varicose veins and helped to tighten them, encouraging blood to flow up. This usage dates back to ancient times: Butcher's broom's healing properties are noted as far back as 325 B.C. In about A.D. 60, Pliny, a Roman scholar, wrote that swollen veins "become flat again after patients took the powdered root of the whisk broom plant." Indeed butcher's broom contains flavonoids that are heralded as blood vessel strengtheners. They also reduce capillary fragility, making the tiniest blood vessels more resistant to bruises and breakage.

Butcher's broom is useful for other circulatory disorders, too. Compounds in it called saponins make it one of nature's most potent cures for thrombosis (blood clots), phlebitis, and hemorrhoids. These substances stimulate the blood vessels to release the hormone norepinephrine, which constricts the vessels and the capillaries. Constricted capillaries keep fluids from seeping out into body spaces, where they cause swelling and edema. Even edema experienced during pregnancy or from standing for long periods can be alleviated with the use of this herb. In addition, norepinephrine lengthens the time it takes for blood to clot, thus preventing thrombosis that can develop after surgery.

TYPE OF PLANT This perennial evergreen bush grows to 4 feet in height. It has small, waxy green leaves and produces white or pink flowers from fall to spring that turn into red or yellow-red berries. It typically grows in woodlands and can thrive even in poor, rocky soil. Its roots produce rhizomes, which are underground stems with shoots coming out of them.

HOW TO GROW Butcher's broom does well in regular garden soil and can be propagated from seeds or cuttings. It can be purchased from a nursery, where it is often sold as an ornamental under the name of box holly.

HARVESTING Harvest leaves when the plant begins to flower; use them fresh or dried. Take roots or rhizomes in the fall; use dried. The berries are not used.

PREPARATION AND DOSAGE Make tea from this herb, drinking up to 3 cups per day or ½ teaspoon tincture per day. It is often combined with other herbs that improve circulation.

Ointments or suppositories are used to treat hemorrhoids. Consult a physician knowledgeable about botanicals for more information.

PRECAUTIONS Butcher's broom can raise blood pressure; avoid this herb if you have high blood pressure. If you're pregnant, check with a qualified practitioner before using butcher's broom.

ALSO KNOWN AS **pot marigold, this flower's bright yellow and orange flowers yield essential oils containing saponins and flavonoids that promote the healing of cuts, burns, and rashes.**

HEALING PROPERTIES Use a strong tea of calendula petals to gently wash skin irritations. The cool tea will bring quick, temporary relief and speed healing. As a salve it is helpful for chapped lips and diaper rash. It is reputed to be particularly helpful for childhood illnesses with fever and rash.

Calendula tea is good for the mouth, too. It can be used as a mouthwash and to help heal tooth and gum infections. Gargle with it to relieve a sore throat and tonsillitis.

Calendula's mild antimicrobial activity and vulnerary (wound healing) agents will clear up vaginal infections when the tea is used in a vaginal douche. Used in a sitz bath, calendula soothes hemorrhoids and post-partum discomfort.

When the opportunistic yeast *Candida albicans* overgrows, it causes thrush in the mouth or a yeast infection in the vagina. Both of these conditions may sometimes be successfully treated with washes of calendula. For thrush, use a tincture diluted with an equal amount of distilled water. Swab the affected area.

Less commonly, calendula is used internally. Drinking its tea may help stomach ulcers and bladder infections. It improves digestion and increases urination. Calendula also has mild diaphoretic properties and may be helpful during a cold.

Diaphoretics increase body temperature leading to increased sweating and, it is believed, increased immune function. However, other herbs such as yarrow and elder flower are much better diaphoretics. Researchers believe certain compounds in calendula may have cancer-fighting abilities; research is just beginning.

Although calendula is a safe and effective skin remedy, there is little modern research supporting its efficacy.

TYPE OF PLANT Calendula is an annual flower reaching 1–2 feet in height. It grows rapidly and blooms profusely all summer. Although often called pot marigold, it is not a true marigold.

HOW TO GROW Calendula grows worldwide. Its seeds can be sown directly into the garden or indoors about two months before the date of the last frost. It prefers warm weather and will bloom until frost arrives. Plant in an area that gets full sun and has well-drained soil. Insects love this plant; you may need to take steps to control them.

HARVESTING Pick flowers in their prime—fully opened but not starting to deteriorate.

PREPARATION AND DOSAGE
Flowers can be dried whole, or you can remove just the petals. Spread them on a screen in a thin layer. Gently turn and mix the petals occasionally while drying to prevent mold.

For a skin wash, make a strong tea by pouring boiling water over the dried flowers or petals. To make a poultice, mash fresh flowers and apply externally where needed. Tincture can be taken internally, up to 1 teaspoon three times per day.

PRECAUTIONS If treating a wound that is open or oozing, use calendula only in a watery formula, such as tea. Wait until a scab has formed or stitches have been removed to apply oil-based preparations.

This herb has a good safety record. It is considered non-toxic.

CHAMOMILE

CHAMOMILE IS A PRETTY herb with a wide variety of uses. It has anti-inflammatory, antispasmodic, and antimicrobial properties and is gentle enough to use with babies and children as well as adults. Chamomile is valuable in the practice of aromatherapy, too, as it calms and lifts the spirits.

HEALING PROPERTIES Chamomile helps treat a variety of gastrointestinal problems. It reduces cramping and spastic pain in the bowels and also relieves excessive gas and bloating in the intestines. It may help prevent or heal ulcers, according to clinical studies in Germany, and treats acute stomach inflammation (gastritis). Some people have found chamomile useful for treating irritable bowel syndrome and colitis.

This herb is an antispasmodic, relaxing muscles including those that line blood vessels. This makes chamomile effective at relieving headaches as well as stomach and intestinal cramps and menstrual cramps.

Chamomile is also an anti-inflammatory and reduces swelling. Inflamed or sunburned skin responds well to chamomile treatment, as does puffiness around the eyes. Clinical trials support the use of chamomile in the treatment of mouth inflammation after chemotherapy or radiation therapy.

German studies in humans confirm that chamomile helps heal wounds. The flowers' essential oils are mildly antimicrobial and can be used to help clean wounds and kill bacteria that cause infection. Taken as a tea with other antimicrobials, this herb can help fight infections.

Chamomile calms the nerves of babies and adults alike. Constituents in chamomile have been shown to bind to the same receptor in the brain as such potent drugs as Valium. However, chamomile has much milder calming effects and there is no risk of addiction. It helps ease children into sleep, and they usually like its pleasant flavor. If you are under stress, sip chamomile tea throughout the day.

Aromatherapy uses chamomile not only to relieve tension, but also to quell anger and depression. If you feel grumpy, discontented, or impatient, this herb might lift your spirits. People who are overly sensitive, self-absorbed, and rarely satisfied can benefit from chamomile's essential oils. No scientific studies have confirmed these uses.

TYPE OF PLANT The two most common types are German chamomile, which is a dainty annual, and Roman chamomile, which is a hearty perennial often used as a ground cover. Both types have very fine leaves.

Chamomile's tiny flowers look like white daisies and give off an apple aroma. It grows widely throughout North America, but there are many look-alikes. Both German and Roman chamomile have stronger medicinal properties than English chamomile, with German chamomile having the most potent essential oils.

HOW TO GROW Seeds need to be planted early in the spring. If using transplants, use at least several plants to make a show.

Otherwise, the plants are so small they'll get lost in the garden landscape. Plant in an area that gets full sun and is relatively dry. Chamomile does not require nutrient-rich soil.

HARVESTING Harvest chamomile's many tiny flowers when they are fully open, preferably early in the day.

PREPARATION AND DOSAGE Spread flowers on a screen to dry, or hang entire plants upside down and remove the flowers after drying.

Pleasant tasting chamomile tea can be used as a beverage as often as you like. Steep 1 tablespoon of dried flowers in 1 cup of water for 15 minutes. For digestive problems, use about ½ cup five times per day.

As a tincture, use up to 1½ teaspoons one to three times per day. This herb is also useful as a poultice: Mash the flowers with a fork and apply to inflamed or bruised areas.

Use chamomile flowers in an aroma lamp, sachets, or potpourri for its aromatherapy effects. A few drops of essential oil can be added to massage oils, lotions, or bathwater.

PRECAUTIONS Those with allergies to ragweed and related plants have a slight chance of being allergic to chamomile. Using chamomile during pregnancy is not problematic.

DANDELION

THIS WEED OFFERS an abundance of vitamins A, C, and K; the minerals calcium, iron, and zinc; and carotenoids. Used for centuries as a digestive aid and for liver support, it has several substances that stimulate the liver and help it filter impurities from the blood.

HEALING PROPERTIES Dandelion root is excellent at stimulating digestion because of a bitter substance called taraxacin. Bitter substances promote the flow of bile from the liver and hydrochloric acid secretion from the stomach. Dandelion also contains choline, another liver stimulant. Since dandelion improves digestion, it also enables the body to absorb nutrients and eliminate wastes more efficiently.

Dandelion leaf is a useful diuretic that contains a large amount of potassium. Many diuretics flush the body of potassium, which

can potentially be dangerous. Researchers equate dandelion's diuretic properties with the prescription drug furosemide in animal studies. Diuretics may result in lower blood pressure and less premenstrual bloat.

The root of the dandelion, when collected in the fall, contains the starches inulin and levulin. The white, sticky resin you see when breaking a leaf, stem, or root can be applied at least twice daily to warts to help remove them.

TYPE OF PLANT Dandelion is a perennial herb often considered a weed. It grows easily almost everywhere and happily takes over an entire area if given the chance. It flowers in late spring, with flowers closing during the night. It produces a long taproot.

How to Grow The better question might be how not to grow! Dandelion's puffballs blow apart in the wind and are an excellent self-seeding mechanism, often making them an uninvited guest. Sow seeds in the spring. It likes full sun and rich soil, but will tolerate most conditions. It may be wise to put dandelions in an area in which you can keep them somewhat contained.

Harvesting If harvesting dandelions from the wild or from a neighbor's yard, be sure no chemicals have been applied to the plants—you can't tell by looking.

Leaves are considered a spring green. Flowers are harvested in late spring and throughout the summer. Dig roots in the fall.

Preparation and Dosage All parts of this plant—leaves, flowers, and roots—are useful.

Wash dandelion leaves thoroughly, then steam them as you do other greens or sautée them in sesame oil with mushrooms.

Blanch leaves to reduce bitterness, then add to tossed salads. Use in soups to boost the mineral content of your broth. Use fresh or freshly dried leaves for tinctures.

The flowers can be made into wine. Leaves and roots are used for tea; the leaves are more of a diuretic than the roots. Drink up to 5 cups per day of tea or up to $\frac{1}{2}$ teaspoon tincture three times per day.

All parts can be used fresh or dried, but need to be used fairly promptly after drying. This is especially true for the leaves.

Precautions Avoid dandelions if you have too much stomach acid, ulcers, diarrhea, irritable bowel syndrome, or ulcerative colitis.

The root contains a white latex substance that causes skin irritations as well as digestive disturbances.

ECHINACEA

COMMONLY CALLED purple coneflower, this lovely flowering herb boosts your immune system. It helps prevent and treat colds and flu. Take it the minute you feel something "coming on," or take it continuously. It can also help your body seek and destroy cancer cells.

HEALING PROPERTIES Traditionally, this potent herb was used by Native Americans and settlers to fight off many illnesses. It fell out of favor with the advent of pharmaceuticals but is now being rediscovered and studied. It's a very popular healing herb in Germany. Researchers have found that it jump-starts the immune system by increasing the number and function of white blood cells that rid the body of infectious microbes. Additionally, it may raise the body's production of interferon, another immune substance, though human studies have yet to confirm this finding.

With properties like this, you can't lose if you need to fight off a cold or flu. Numerous clinical trials have shown that echinacea can prevent and shorten the duration of these viral illnesses.

For treatment of infections including those of the ear and bladder, consult a knowledgeable practitioner before using echinacea to treat them. Treatment with echinacea is even being tried for chronic fatigue syndrome and cancer—with promising results.

Echinacea may also be helpful for skin conditions such as eczema and boils. When taken internally, it supports collagen, the body's base for skin, muscles, bones, and connective tissues.

Echinacea has also been suggested as a treatment for sunburn.

TYPE OF PLANT Echinacea is a tall perennial with purplish-pink flowers that look somewhat daisylike with cone-shaped flower heads. Its stems are stout and bristly with pale to dark green leaves. *Echinacea purpurea* is the variety most often used for medicinal purposes. *Echinacea angustifolia* may have slightly different actions, but is often used along with E. *purpurea*. No studies have definitively shown that one species is better than another.

How to Grow Sow seeds in early spring. Provide an area preferably with full sun; light shade works too, but the medicine won't be as strong. Echinacea likes well-drained soil. Be on the lookout for leaf spot or Japanese beetles. Mulch well through the winter. About every four years, dig up echinacea to divide the plant, then replant in rich soil.

Harvesting Roots, seeds, and leaves are used therapeutically. Harvest roots in the fall, when the plant begins to die back.

Replant the crown. They are currently being over-harvested from the wild, so please grow your own.

Preparation and Dosage Dry or tincture the root, or make tea. Take doses three to ten times a day when fighting off an illness. Use up to 1 teaspoon tincture for each dose for several days, then reduce the dosage. For best results, use a tincture; powdered roots are only effective if they are less than several months old. The best way to tell if the roots are fresh is by taste; they should increase salivation and create a tingling sensation in your mouth.

Precautions If you have HIV or AIDS, consult a qualified health care provider before taking this herb. Otherwise, this herb is considered safe. Be sure to consult a physician if you have a persistent condition.

ELDERBERRY

THE ELEGANT elderberry's flowers and berries have medicinal value. They have long been used to cure the flu and more recently to stimulate immune function and enhance the cardiovascular system.

HEALING PROPERTIES Elderberry flowers are known for reducing inflammation, swelling, and puffiness. A cold infusion used as an eyewash treats conjunctivitis and puffiness. Drinking elderberry flower tea may break up bronchial and upper-respiratory congestion. Gargling with elder flower infusion helps a sore throat or tonsillitis. Infusions of the flowers are also a useful treatment for hay fever.

Research shows that elderberries have antiviral activity. It is hoped they can be added to the growing arsenal of substances that are believed to inhibit viruses such as HIV and herpes. Other studies have found the berries to reduce fever, coughs, and even muscle pain. They also gently stimulate digestion.

Only the blue and black elderberries should be used. Large quantities of the red berries are potentially unsafe and have an unpleasant taste. Red berries contain the same compounds found in apricot kernels that are used by some to fight cancer. It's probably safe to eat 3 berries a day.

The richly colored berries are full of flavonoids, making them effective at keeping arteries and capillaries healthy and resistant to breakage, leakage, and bruising. The flowers are a potent diaphoretic—they stimulate a mild fever, which leads to sweating and immune stimulation. This may partially explain its benefit for colds and flu. The berries also stimulate circulation and are rich in vitamin C.

The elderberry may be a good flu remedy due to its ability to stimulate the immune system. Syrup made from this little berry helped two-thirds of the people in one study recover from the flu in only two days.

Blue or black berries are also a good source of iron. In traditional herbalism they are used to invigorate the elderly and mothers in the postpartum period.

TYPE OF PLANT The deciduous perennial elderberry shrub grows as high as 50 feet, often looking more like a tree than a bush. It spreads graceful branches to 20 feet in diameter and may take over more territory than you had planned. It produces cream-colored to light yellow fragrant flowers that turn into clusters of small, smooth purplish-black berries.

HOW TO GROW Although elderberry can be grown from seed, it is easiest to propagate it from suckers or cuttings of adult plants. It likes rich, moist soil and full sun but will tolerate partial shade. Because it spreads, start it in a place where you don't mind having a lot of shrubbery.

HARVESTING Flowers should be picked when they are fully developed. Harvest berries when they are deeply colored and juicy.

PREPARATION AND DOSAGE
Flowers may be used fresh or dried. Only berries that are purplish-blue-black in color can be eaten. Large quantities may have a laxative effect and cause indigestion. However, cooking the berries takes care of this problem. Cook the berries before making juice.

You may drink up to 3 cups per day of elderberry flower tea. If using tincture, limit your intake to 1 teaspoon per day.

PRECAUTION Do not use the leaves, bark, or roots of the elderberry internally, as they are slightly toxic. Remember to avoid the variety of elderberry that produces red berries; they should not be eaten.

FENNEL

A FEATHERY, WHISPERY-LOOKING HERB, fennel has been used since the time of ancient Greece to treat a variety of maladies. From improving digestion to increasing milk flow in new mothers, the Greeks used fennel for young and old alike.

HEALING PROPERTIES During the Middle Ages this herb helped relieve many digestive problems. Early physicians also prescribed it as a remedy for ailments such as poor eyesight, weight loss, and gout, to name a few. Today herbalists find many of the same uses for fennel, and science is uncovering its healing compounds.

Fennel is an effective carminative. This means it helps to relieve gas and bloating in the stomach and intestines. It soothes a stomachache while dispelling the problematic gas. Even infants with colic can benefit from fennel. This herb may relax muscles in the intestinal walls, alleviating cramps. Fennel also promotes digestion.

This herb has mild diuretic properties. It might tone and decrease inflammation in the urinary tract.

Nursing mothers like fennel, as it increases milk flow. This action is possibly due to fennel's mild estrogenlike effects.

A good antispasmodic, fennel relaxes the smooth muscles that line artery walls and respiratory passages. This means fennel helps cure bronchitis, asthma, and other respiratory ailments, including coughs.

Nutritionally speaking, this herb is rich in minerals such as calcium and potassium as well as vitamins. Flavonoids in the seeds promote a healthy heart and arteries, although few people eat enough to get very many flavonoids from them.

TYPE OF PLANT Fennel is a tall, hardy perennial. It has feathery leaves and looks similar to its smaller cousin, dill. It flowers from June until October. Its stems, stalks, and seeds have a pleasant licorice or anise taste.

HOW TO GROW This herb is easy to care for. It doesn't mind full sun or partial shade. Average soil will do, although it does prefer it a bit alkaline. Sow seeds in late fall or early spring. Plant in an area where it will get shelter from strong winds, as its stems are fragile and can easily be blown over.

HARVESTING Both foliage and seeds of this plant are used. Trim leaves any time. The entire plant can be harvested right before it blooms. Hang to dry.

Seeds can be harvested either when they are fully mature yet still green or after they turn brown. Cut down plants and cover seed heads with paper bags to catch the seeds. Hang them to dry.

PREPARATION AND DOSAGE Foliage and seeds can both be used in cooking. Leaves are tasty in salads or as a garnish. Treat stems like celery, but expect a different taste! Fennel bulbs, the base of the plant, can be eaten raw or lightly steamed. The seeds are commonly used as a spice. Slightly crush the seeds before using to get the best flavor as well as medicinal value.

Make an infusion for topical application or to drink as tea when using the foliage. The seeds can be gently simmered or steeped in a closed container for 20 minutes or more.

PRECAUTION Some people may be allergic to fennel, although this is rare. This is a very safe food-level herb.

FEVERFEW

FEVERFEW IS WELL-KNOWN, both in folk wisdom and modern science, for its ability to prevent headaches, especially the dreaded migraine headache. Feverfew relaxes blood vessels inside the brain, preventing expansion. It also inhibits certain substances such as antihistamines that cause inflammation and signal pain.

HEALING PROPERTIES The active ingredient in feverfew is called parthenolide. It stops blood vessel spasms, which in turn protects against headaches. It is also an anti-inflammatory and appears to prevent excessive stickiness of blood platelets, believed to play a role in the development of a migraine. If people taking feverfew do get a headache, it is often less severe than usual. The herb may also reduce blood pressure, and people report feeling better emotionally after taking it.

But that's not all feverfew can do. It may also be effective against headaches that are caused by fluctuating hormones and fluid retention—both of which are conditions experienced by many women during the premenstrual portion of their monthly menstrual cycle.

Although feverfew was historically used to help arthritis, a clinical trial in patients with one specific type of rheumatoid arthritis found it to be relatively ineffective for this purpose.

Feverfew is also used to alleviate menstrual cramps and to reduce inflammation of joints and tissues. It may be effective at breaking a fever in some people, but not in those who are weakened, especially the very young, the very old, and those with a serious, chronic disease.

TYPE OF PLANT Feverfew is a perennial or biennial growing throughout North America. It has many stems that produce small white flowers with yellow centers that resemble daisies.

HOW TO GROW Seeds for feverfew can be sown directly

into the garden in the spring. Mature plants can also be divided in springtime. Cuttings may be done either in the spring or fall. This herb is easy to grow in average soil with full sun to partial shade.

HARVESTING It is feverfew's leaves that are used for medicinal purposes, although research is finding that the flowers may also be effective. Typically the leaves are best snipped just before the plant flowers. Collect flowers when in bloom but not past their prime.

PREPARATION AND DOSAGE

Feverfew leaves can be dried and made into tinctures and infusions or put into capsules. Making a tincture is not a good way to preserve the healing properties of feverfew. Clinical studies using alcohol extracts have never shown feverfew to be effective, while those using whole leaves have all shown it to work well.

Perhaps the best way to enjoy the benefits of feverfew is to eat the leaves raw. It is in the undried state that the active ingredient, parthenolide, is most likely to remain intact. Eat 1–4 washed leaves per day, but do not exceed 5 leaves per day. Due to their bitterness, you may wish to combine feverfew leaves with other greens. If your mouth becomes irritated, mix the leaves with other food to limit contact and irritation.

To make an infusion, pour 1 cup boiling water over 1 tablespoon dried leaves and let set for 10 minutes. Mix feverfew with pleasantly flavored herbs, using up to 3 cups per day. Infusions are not likely to be effective in preventing headaches.

PRECAUTION Raw leaves can irritate the mucous membranes of the mouth or cause stomach upset. Tinctures and capsules do not cause mouth irritation.

Feverfew's ability to relax blood vessels means it might increase bleeding during menstruation. Pregnant women should avoid feverfew, especially during the first trimester, as it may cause miscarriage.

Feverfew should be kept out of the reach of children. Long-term effects are not yet known about this herb; more research is needed to determine its safety if taken over long periods. Studies lasting 11 months in humans have shown it does not cause precancerous changes in DNA.

Feverfew is a very potent herb. Although no specific information is available on overdose, you are strongly discouraged from taking larger than recommended doses.

SCENTED GERANIUMS, particularly the rose variety, are used primarily for their scent in both men's and women's personal care products, lotions, and splashes or to lightly scent a room. This herb carries relaxing and astringent properties.

HEALING PROPERTIES

Aromatherapists use geranium in small quantities to induce relaxation and emotional balance. The essential oils in the leaves alleviate nervous tension, fear, and depression. This herb brings a sense of calm and, in some cases, stimulates sensual feelings. During menopause the aroma may help balance hormones. Used in an aromatherapy lamp, it is also useful for repelling insects.

One of the phytochemicals in geranium, geraniol, is used as an antiseptic. It also has astringent properties, making it useful for treating cuts and other wounds.

Used topically, the oil of these scented leaves may be helpful for skin disorders such as eczema, shingles, or the inflammation of acne. It also reduces the inflammation of stomatitis, an inflammatory disease of the mouth. Some herbalists also use scented geranium to treat herpes virus as well as ringworm and lice.

TYPE OF PLANT

What is commonly called a geranium in this country is actually a pelargonium. It is the scented varieties that are used for the purposes described above. The pink flowers of these plants have no fragrance, but if you brush against its leaves, you'll understand why it is called "scented geranium." *Pelargonium graveolens*, for instance, which has profuse foliage and a modest bloom, has a rose scent. *P. crispum* has lemon-scented leaves, *P. grossularioides* smells like coconut, *P. nervosum* carries a lime fragrance, and *P. fragrans* smells like nutmeg. The peppermint-scented *P. tomentosum* is one of the most commonly grown scented geraniums.

These plants grow about 2 feet in height with a 1-foot spread. If nighttime temperatures do not climb above 60°F, the plants will bloom all summer long. If your climate has warm nights, they will stop blooming mid-season and pick up again when cooler nights arrive.

Although geraniums are perennials, they are typically grown as annuals.

HOW TO GROW These flowering plants are very tender and cannot tolerate frost. Put them in a lightly shaded area in rich, loamy soil that is well-drained. Start plants from cuttings in spring or summer, then transplant to the garden in several weeks.

HARVESTING Harvest scented geranium leaves at any time. If you wish to use the flowers, pick them as soon as they bloom.

PREPARATION AND DOSAGE Use the leaves of this herb fresh or dried. They make a flavorful tea or can be used in cooking. Add cut leaves to fruit salads, jellies, cookies, or use to flavor and adorn desserts. Place leaves in the bottom of a greased cake pan, then add batter and bake. Turn the cake out of the pan to enjoy the decorative leaves.

Rose geranium is used for its aromatherapy value. Add leaves for scent and flowers for visual appeal to potpourri and sachets. Essential oil drops can be mixed with skin care creams or lotions, put in a carrier oil for massage, or used as a facial steam to cleanse and heal the skin.

PRECAUTIONS There are no known precautions, side effects, or toxicities associated with scented geraniums.

THE LEAVES of this ancient tree have profound healing properties. They possess not only antioxidants but other phytochemicals, too. These substances thin the blood, help cells communicate, and dilate blood vessels.

HEALING PROPERTIES When vessels expand, they carry more blood rich in oxygen, vitamins, minerals, and beneficial plant chemicals. The more of these nutrients organs get, the better they perform. For instance, when the brain receives plenty of nutrient-rich blood, many people report improved memory and less depression. When eyes get all the nutrient-dense blood they need, there is less incidence of macular degeneration. Impotence, too, is helped by increased blood flow.

Some of ginkgo's substances also prevent blood platelets from sticking together, reducing clot formation and possibly preventing heart disease and strokes.

Ginkgo's antioxidants wreak havoc on free radicals, those cell-damaging molecules that may be partially responsible for many of the signs of aging as well as cancer and cataracts. Ginkgo's dilation properties, as well as its ability to decrease the production of chemicals that cause spasms, have made it useful for treating asthma in some children.

TYPE OF PLANT Ginkgo biloba is a deciduous tree that grows to 100 feet with a 20-foot spread. Its leaves are an attractive fan shape. Female trees produce grape-size, yellowish–orange-colored fruit that smell like rancid butter when decomposing. Plant only male trees to avoid the odiferous fruit. Ginkgos grow throughout most regions of the United States.

HOW TO GROW Ginkgos are easy trees to grow. They are resistant to diseases, insects, pollution, and even drought. Young trees from a nursery should be planted in the spring in an area with well-drained soil.

HARVESTING Leaves are the only part of the ginkgo that is commonly used in this country. Gather during late summer or early fall, ideally after the color has turned on the tips only.

PREPARATION AND DOSAGE Dry the leaves of the ginkgo to make a tincture or tea out of them. Limit use to 1 teaspoon of tincture per day in divided doses, such as ½ teaspoon twice a day or ⅓ teaspoon three times a day.

Commercially prepared capsules are recommended for two reasons: compounds that cause unwanted side effects when highly concentrated are removed and the active flavonoid content has been standardized. Any form may cause headache and stomach or intestinal discomfort. Choose capsules that have a standardized 24 percent flavonoid and 6 percent terpene lactone content. Typical effective dosages used in research are 120 mg taken two or three times per day.

PRECAUTIONS Since ginkgo increases blood circulation in the brain, it could worsen certain kinds of headaches and also increase the risk of one type of stroke. In addition, capsules of standardized extracts may cause excessive bleeding in people taking blood-thinning medications if they injure themselves. Tinctures and teas have not been reported to cause this problem. Large doses may cause irritability and gastrointestinal upset, including diarrhea, nausea, and vomiting.

Ginkgo appears to be safe for most people. In Europe, however, it's offered only as a prescription medication. Check with an experienced health care provider before taking this herb.

THIS HERB IS a strong antimicrobial with mild anti-inflammatory properties. One of its active ingredients may be able to increase white blood cell activity. Another active substance tones muscles.

HEALING PROPERTIES Goldenseal contains a compound called berberine, which is credited with the herb's antimicrobial effects, although two other antimicrobial alkaloids, hydrastine and canadine, are also thought to be important. Goldenseal can treat a variety of internal and external infections, including those of the mouth, skin, stomach, throat, and vagina. Goldenseal infusions can be used as a mouthwash for the oral cavity, while capsules can help internally. Use a wash to swab wounds and infected eyes, to treat an ear infection, or as a douche for a vaginal infection.

The alkaloid berbamine, a close cousin of berberine, holds promise as an adjunct to cancer therapy. Researchers in China have used it to boost white blood cell counts during cancer treatment. It may also be effective in treating cancers of the brain and skin. Scientists theorize that goldenseal's immune-stimulating qualities may help the body's defenses destroy abnormal cells, while its astringent properties heal inflamed cells.

Unfortunately, no scientific studies have been done using whole goldenseal. However, many studies have been done on its isolated alkaloid berberine. This accounts for only a part of goldenseal's activity.

TYPE OF PLANT Goldenseal is a small perennial in the Ranunculaceae family. It has bristly stems growing from rhizomes beneath the soil. Each stem produces only a couple of maple-shaped leaves. A white flower appears in late spring to produce an orange-red berry.

HOW TO GROW It may be difficult to grow goldenseal from seeds. Mature plants can be divided or purchased through a mail-order nursery. In the wild, goldenseal prefers a damp, rich, woodland. This herb is on the endangered list due to overharvesting of wild plants. It is difficult to grow and takes about five years before it can be harvested.

HARVESTING After five years, the root, which is the only part of this plant that is used, is large enough to harvest. Take roots late in the fall. The roots of Oregon grape and barberry, both much more common plants in the wild and in landscapes, contain the same berberine as goldenseal.

PREPARATION AND DOSAGE

Slowly dry the harvested roots. They are very bitter, so are not good candidates for tea. Instead, make a tincture or put ground root in capsules. However, people with poor digestion would benefit from drinking bitter teas such as goldenseal before meals.

Take tincture frequently—every hour or two—at the onset of illness. Use ¼–½ teaspoon each time, diminishing in frequency after a few days.

If using capsules, again take frequently in the beginning: 1 or 2 capsules every 2–4 hours. Reduce frequency after two or three days, then stop after infection has cleared.

Children and older adults should take smaller doses.

PRECAUTIONS Goldenseal contains alkaloids, potentially harmful compounds, so avoid during pregnancy. Hydrastine, the substance that tones muscles, is toxic in very large doses (more than the doses recommended here) and can raise blood pressure. If you have high blood pressure, heart disease, or glaucoma, do not take goldenseal unless a qualified health care professional recommends it and monitors you.

As an antibiotic, goldenseal may kill off not only unwanted bacteria, but also the good, friendly bacteria that live in the intestine. This has not been documented in scientific studies, but it is a theoretical risk. Still, it may be advisable while using goldenseal and for a week or so afterward to eat plenty of yogurt with live cultures, or take supplements of *Lactobacillus acidophilus* to reestablish beneficial bacteria in the intestines.

Goldenseal used as a tincture or wash can stain clothing and skin yellow.

It is not recommended to be used longer than 10 days.

HAWTHORN

HAWTHORN IS a scientifically proven heart tonic that improves heart tone, protects blood vessels, enhances circulation, normalizes blood pressure, and mildly reduces cholesterol levels. It may also normalize a rapid or irregular heartbeat, although this action awaits further research.

HEALING PROPERTIES Hawthorn is useful for toning the heart muscle. It dilates blood vessels, allowing better blood flow throughout the body. This enables the heart to receive all the nutrient-rich blood and oxygen it needs, thus improving heart function. This herb is therefore used to treat heart conditions such as angina (chest pain) and a weak or enlarged heart. Many clinical studies have shown that hawthorn helps people with congestive heart failure. It is also an effective adjunct treatment for high blood pressure.

Chock-full of chemical compounds such as the flavonoids anthocyanidin and proanthocyanidin, hawthorn protects blood vessels from oxidizers such as cigarette smoke, air pollution, certain food additives, and other chemicals. These pollutants can trigger a chain of events that lead to plaque build-up in the arteries. Hawthorn extract puts a stop to that. It also strengthens and improves the integrity of blood vessels, helping them become more elastic, avoiding hardening of the arteries. Although studies are lacking to show how effective hawthorn is at this in humans, animal studies have shown some effect.

Hawthorn used on a regular basis helps the heart to withstand oxygen deprivation to a greater extent than usual when under stress. This means that if a person who routinely used hawthorn suffered a heart attack, the heart might not suffer severe damage.

TYPE OF PLANT Hawthorn is a perennial with thorns and white flower clusters that turn into bright maroon-colored berries. Its flowers appear in May, and the berries usually ripen in October. There are more than 900 varieties in North America, ranging from shrubs to deciduous trees. The researched varieties are native to Europe and can reach 25 feet in height with a 10-foot spread. Hawthorn can grow in most temperate areas, especially in deciduous woods.

HOW TO GROW Sow seeds in spring or transplant small-sized trees from a nursery. Some varieties must be grafted or budded. Plant in an area with full sun and slightly alkaline, rich, moist soil. Hawthorn is prone to aphids, other insects, and fungus.

HARVESTING Gather flowers in spring with a couple of leaves; collect berries in the fall. It is best to harvest both so they can eventually be used together.

PREPARATION AND DOSAGE Prepare tinctures from the flowers and leaves; make berry tincture in the fall and combine them to benefit from the healing compounds each contains. Use ½–1 teaspoon up to five times per day or drink up to 5 cups tea per day.

Berries can also be eaten raw or made into jam or syrup.

PRECAUTION Hawthorn is considered safe even for long-term use. However, if you take medications, particularly heart medications, it is important that you inform your health care provider. Hawthorn may increase the action of certain medications. If you take hawthorn along with a normal amount of a prescription drug, you may end up with an overdose and severe problems, although this has not been scientifically documented.

HORSERADISH

THIS PUNGENT HERB is very effective at breaking up and alleviating mucus congestion. It clears nasal and sinus passages rapidly. For centuries, horseradish has been used not only as a condiment, but also for these medicinal purposes. It has mild antibiotic properties, making it useful for treating sinus infections or wounds.

HEALING PROPERTIES If you're prone to developing a sinus infection every time you get a cold, you should develop a taste for horseradish. A simple cold can easily turn into a painful sinus infection if mucus gets thick and stagnates, making a perfect environment for bacteria to breed. Horseradish's powerful oils thin mucus, making it watery and allowing the body to get rid of it. No modern studies have documented the efficacy of horseradish for treating any infection.

Horseradish cuts congestion not only in the sinuses, but also in the lungs. Again, it thins the mucus so the body can expel it. You may actually experience more drainage, but this is a positive indication that the body is ridding itself of wastes.

Horseradish helps out with bladder infections, too. It is a natural antibiotic and it stimulates the production of urine, making it a good adjunct to treatment for urinary tract infections.

This herb also stimulates digestion, aiding in the digestion of rich meals.

TYPE OF PLANT Horseradish is a perennial that is easily grown in the garden. It produces a long, white root.

HOW TO GROW This herb is propagated by root cuttings taken early in the spring. From a mature plant, cut portions of the root 8–9 inches in length, each with a bud. Plant about 12–15 inches deep in moist, heavy soil. Horseradish likes full sun. Plant it where you don't mind it spreading; it is difficult to get rid of once established.

HARVESTING Harvest roots late in the fall. Store whole roots in a cool, dark place covered with dry sand. They will stay fresh for several months. Alternatively, store fresh roots in a resealable plastic bag in the refrigerator, where they will keep the same length of time.

PREPARATION AND DOSAGE This herb is safe for long-term use.

Preserve horseradish by grating the root and putting it in vinegar or lemon juice. If exposed to air for long, its potent mustardlike oil disintegrates. The volatile oils make your eyes water, so be careful preparing it; you may prefer to use it as a food. Use preserved horseradish within three months. If using dried horseradish, soak it in a small amount of water at least 30 minutes before needed.

You can add sweetener to preserved horseradish and spread thinly on crackers. Stir horseradish and honey into 2 tablespoons of water and drink, or steep 1 teaspoon fresh grated horseradish in hot water. Add other herbs, sweeteners, or flavors such as citrus to make the tea more palatable.

If using tincture, take ¼–½ teaspoon straight or in warm water. Repeat hourly to clear congestion.

You can apply a horseradish poultice to wounds, but discontinue if skin irritation develops.

PRECAUTIONS Large amounts of this potent herb may cause nausea, vomiting, or headache. If you have trouble digesting members of the cabbage family, avoid this herb; even a small amount may trigger nausea. Used topically, its strong oils may cause inflammation or rash.

HORSETAIL

HORSETAIL IS a traditional treatment for bladder and kidney conditions, and it has been used to strengthen bones. It may help stop external and internal bleeding and reduce an enlarged prostate. Very few studies, however, have confirmed the traditional wisdom, although horsetail does hold promise as a treatment for all these conditions.

HEALING PROPERTIES Horsetail tones the bladder, possibly preventing nighttime incontinence in adults and helping children who wet the bed. If you are bothered by a constant urge to urinate, this herb may help alleviate that sensation. Horsetail is also used to clear up bladder infections when part of a comprehensive program that is overseen by a health practitioner knowledgeable about herbal medicine.

This herb has questionable diuretic properties, but some people benefit from it, gaining relief from swelling in the legs and feet.

This herb's high mineral content may make it great for bone health. Drinking horsetail tea daily may help broken bones mend well. The high silica content may increase absorption and metabolism of calcium. This herb may also guard against atherosclerosis, the fatty buildup in arteries.

Horsetail can be used as a conditioning hair rinse. Its saponins create lather, phytochemicals called flavone glycosides stimulate blood vessels in the scalp, and silica gives added body to your hair.

TYPE OF PLANT Perennial and persistent, this is one of the oldest plant species known. During its first stage it produces a greenish stalk with brown stripes, about 4—8 inches tall. As the season continues, the stalk gives way to whorls of thin, wispy, fernlike leaves, growing up to 1½ feet in height. It grows in moist woods and along roads.

HOW TO GROW If you see a wild patch of horsetail, dig it up and divide the roots. Otherwise, purchase it from a nursery. This herb likes partial shade and slightly acidic, moist soil. Plant in a place where you don't mind its spreading nature, as it is difficult to eradicate.

HARVESTING Early spring is when the young horsetail shoots are at their best. Gather when stalks are 4—5 inches in length and have not yet started to leaf out.

Harvest the branches during early spring only, as they may contain a nerve toxin, equisetene, which increases in quantity as the plant matures.

PREPARATION AND DOSAGE Eat stalks as you do asparagus—

steam them lightly for a great mineral boost.

The branches of horsetail can be made into tinctures and infusions. A traditional recipe for making syrup is reported to be the most effective. Drink up to 3 cups of horsetail tea per day.

If using capsules, take only 2 per day.

PRECAUTIONS If you harvest wild horsetail, avoid roadsides or other areas where it may have been chemically treated.

At recommended doses, horsetail is without significant toxicity. Use of species other than *Equisetum arvense* may carry other risks and should be avoided. Do not take horsetail close to the time you've taken the B vitamin thiamin as it may interfere with its metabolism.

HYDRANGEA

THIS BOUNTIFUL-LOOKING BUSH with profuse flower clusters is native to North America. It was used medicinally by American Indians for everything from wound and burn treatment to sore or sprained muscles and stomach ailments. It contains many beneficial phytochemicals.

HEALING PROPERTIES Hydrangea contains several substances, called saponins, resins, and glycosides, which all have healing properties. Hydrangin, one of its glycosides, helps account for hydrangea's ability to treat bladder and urinary tract infections and other urinary tract inflammations. This plant is a diuretic, which encourages urinary flow. As a result, it is good at preventing kidney stones and helps pass stones that already exist. All of these conditions are quite painful.

This plant's diuretic properties may also make it useful for treating edema, the overaccumulation of fluid in tissues. Fluid must get back into the bloodstream so the kidney can excrete it as urine. Diuretics help this process occur.

Hydrangea is also frequently used to reduce an enlarged prostate gland. An enlarged gland, while not indicative of cancer, causes pain, discomfort, and difficult urination. This plant is often combined with others that reduce prostate inflammation. However, clinical studies have not confirmed this observed result.

TYPE OF PLANT Hydrangea is a large, bushy perennial. It can reach 9 feet in height and 6 feet in diameter. There are many wild and cultivated species.

Typically, flowers can be cream-colored, pink, or blue, depending on the alkalinity of the soil. The large flower clusters bloom from July through September or later. The plant has large green leaves and produces rhizomes, which are roots that run parallel to the surface of the ground instead of straight downward. This bush is sometimes called Seven Barks because it produces seven layers of bark, each a different color. In the eastern portion of the United States, hydrangea grows wild in wooded areas.

HOW TO GROW This bush prefers full sun or partial shade. It likes rich, moist soil. Propagate by taking cuttings or by layering—a process in which a low-growing branch is carefully bent to ground level and covered with soil, leaving at least 5 inches of tip exposed. Soil must be packed tightly to hold the branch. Keep the mound well watered. In several weeks, after the branch has rooted well, it can be snipped from the parent plant and transplanted.

HARVESTING The dried roots and rhizomes of hydrangea are used for medicinal purposes, while its showy flowers are incorporated into craft projects or dried floral arrangements.

Harvest roots in the autumn, when their phytochemical content is at its peak. They get very hard when dried, so clean and cut them while fresh. Gather flowers just before they are in full bloom.

PREPARATION AND DOSAGE Tea made from hydrangea root can be taken in amounts up to 3 cups per day. For tinctures, use ¾ teaspoon three times per day.

Dry the flowers quickly to retain as much color as possible or dry in silica gel.

PRECAUTIONS Consuming large amounts of hydrangea can cause dizziness and indigestion; instead, take smaller doses. The woody parts of the plant may cause a skin reaction upon contact. Do not eat the flowers. There are reports of children becoming ill after eating the buds.

JUNIPER

JUNIPER BERRIES, typically used to make gin, have a much higher and nobler calling. They possess antiseptic qualities that can treat urinary tract infections. Their compounds improve the tone of the bladder, uterus, and muscles. Applied topically, juniper relieves lung congestion and may alleviate skin conditions such as psoriasis.

HEALING PROPERTIES Juniper is a useful diuretic in small doses. It is also mildly antibacterial and therefore makes a handy addition to a treatment plan for urinary tract infections (UTI). Because it is very strong, and because bladder infections can spread to the kidney, juniper and other herbs for the treatment of UTI should be used only under the care of an experienced clinician familiar with herbs. It also may be helpful in the case of bladder prolapse or a weak bladder or urethra.

As people age, they often lose tone in various tissues, muscles, and organs. Juniper may help older adults with chronic diseases such as joint pain, gout, rheumatoid arthritis, and muscle and tendon ailments. It can also tone the uterus to help trigger delayed menstruation.

Juniper stimulates the production of stomach acid, helping to relieve the gas and bloating that result from an insufficient amount of stomach acid.

Used topically, juniper's volatile oils, mixed with other oil and rubbed on the chest, can break up lung congestion and treat coughs. This plant's tars and resins treat psoriasis and other difficult skin conditions, but it should not be used on very sensitive skin.

Aromatherapy uses juniper essential oil to lift the spirits and ease anxiety and weakness. It cleanses the atmosphere of a room, facilitating meditation or other centering activities.

TYPE OF PLANT Junipers are hardy perennials ranging from shrubs to trees. Their needle-shaped leaves are green and prickly. Bluish-purple berries form in the bush's second year. This plant grows throughout North America.

HOW TO GROW Germination from seed can take two or three years, so most people buy nursery stock. Transplant in early spring or fall for best results. Cuttings taken late in the summer will root easily if kept moist. Junipers prefer sandy soil and full sun, but will tolerate almost any condition. To get a crop of berries, grow both male and female plants.

HARVESTING You can use juniper's leaves as well as its berries. Harvest leaves anytime, but you may want to wear gardening gloves because of their prickly nature. Harvest only ripe berries, which take two years to turn dark bluish-purple, in the fall.

PREPARATION AND DOSAGE Dry berries on a screen until black in color; make into a tincture.

Limit juniper tea to 1 cup per day, taking it for only a week and then discontinuing for a week or two, using for a maximum of 6 weeks. Use no more than 10–20 drops of tincture four times per day for no more than four to six weeks.

Add juniper essential oil to a carrier oil such as almond or coconut for a stimulating massage. Essential oil is extracted by steam distillation from dried berries.

PRECAUTIONS Juniper is very potent. It has a bad reputation for damaging the kidneys if used too long or in high doses and for causing miscarriage. However, a thorough search of clinical studies by aromatherapy experts Robert Tisserand and Tony Balacs found that most reported cases of juniper oil poisoning were instead most likely problems with a related but much more toxic plant called savin. Recent animal studies were unable to find any dose of juniper oil or its major active compound, terpinene-4-ol, that caused kidney damage. Nevertheless, people with kidney disease should be careful when using juniper until its safety has been definitively proven. It

should not be used during pregnancy.

Do not exceed the doses noted here unless you are under the close supervision of a qualified health care professional.

Symptoms of overdose include increased stomach acid, vomiting, diarrhea, pain in the intestines or kidney area, blood in the urine, high blood pressure, and rapid heartbeat. Use the essential oil for external purposes only. Discontinue internal or external use if you experience any reactions to this herb.

LAVENDER

THE DELIGHTFUL AROMA of lavender's tall, stately flowers brings peace and calm to the spirit. Studies reveal and confirm the relaxing properties of this herb. But when used topically, lavender has other healing properties, too.

HEALING PROPERTIES Used as a poultice, lavender helps disinfect wounds. It's also able to kill some cold and flu viruses. And if you do get a cold, lavender can alleviate congestion in your head and lungs.

Lavender has mild antispasmodic effects on tense muscles when used in a massage oil. It is also a carminative, relieving gas and bloating in the large intestine. Linalool, one of lavender's volatile oils, has expectorant properties and reduces inflammation in the airways, helping to relax bronchial tubes and make breathing easier. For this reason, it is sometimes used to treat asthma or allergies.

Lavender makes a great addition to such products as lotions, perfumes, hair rinses, and body washes because of its universally pleasing scent, which blends well with other aromas.

One study found that lavender baths were somewhat effective for healing skin tears in women following childbirth. Pain relief was particularly improved in those using real lavender oil.

In aromatherapy, lavender is said to wash away impurities of body and mind. Lavender quiets an overactive mind, inviting sleep.

TYPE OF PLANT Lavender is a bushy perennial that grows 2–6 feet in height. It produces tall flower stalks that typically have clusters of purple flowers, although some species produce white or pink ones. Lavender has contrasting silver-gray leaves. This herb is rather hardy and is grown throughout the United States.

HOW TO GROW Give lavender a spot in the sun with well-drained soil. Like many herbs, it prefers soil that is not particularly rich, doing well in an alkaline environment. Sow seeds in spring or take cuttings before flowering begins. This plant is easy to grow either in the garden or in containers. If you put it in an outdoor container, its pretty show of flowers can be moved to different areas of the garden. Certain species of this plant make a nice edging or low hedge. Check with a nursery, which usually offers transplants, to determine which variety will suit your needs.

HARVESTING Use lavender's leaves, flowers, and branches. Pick flowers just before they bloom, when they are still in the late bud stage. Some people prefer to use only the flowers.

PREPARATION AND DOSAGE Hang lavender branches so that all parts become dry. Lavender is not usually taken internally, although its dried flowers can be made into an infusion. It is typically used for its enchanting aromatic essence. The essential oil makes a soothing addition to bathwater, creams, and salves. As with any essential oil, 1 drop can have quite an effect, and it's easy to overdose with more than 3 drops even in a bathtub full of water. Add a few drops to hot water and inhale the steam to help relieve congestion of the lungs and sinuses.

As a compress, lavender is used to relieve headaches, tired eyes, and skin injuries.

Avoid using synthetic oil; in human studies it has proved ineffective compared to real oil.

PRECAUTIONS Do not use this herb during pregnancy. If lavender's smell is offensive to you, avoid it; it may irritate the nose and cause nausea. Otherwise, lavender is considered to be safe and without side effects.

LEMON BALM

A FRAGRANT HERB used for more than 2,000 years, lemon balm is an effective tranquilizer, generally soothing the entire nervous system. It is an antiviral, too.

HEALING PROPERTIES Lemon balm may relieve nervous tension that stems from long-standing worry, stress, and anxiety. If anxiety causes a headache, depression, exhaustion, upset stomach, or even sluggishness and confusion, try lemon balm. Research shows that this herb, especially when combined with valerian, is highly effective. In fact, it rivals tranquilizers in its healing abilities and has no unwanted side effects. Lemon balm can even calm a nervous stomach and stop minor heart palpitations.

Lemon balm is a useful antiviral herb. It particularly seeks out and destroys the herpes virus. Lemon balm may also combat cold and flu viruses.

This herb has mild antihistamine effects, making it useful for colds and headaches. Research reveals that lemon balm may be an adjunct treatment for hyperthyroidism, although it does not replace medication. Consult a health care professional who is knowledgeable about natural medicine before using lemon balm to treat hyperthyroidism.

Antispasmodic action makes lemon balm a good choice for relieving stomach and intestinal cramps. It is also able to relax blood vessels, which means it may help lower elevated blood pressure.

Externally, a wash of lemon balm may help heal acne sores.

Aromatherapy uses lemon balm as a remedy for insomnia, nightmares, depression, sadness, and anger, although studies have not confirmed its efficacy. It is safe for children both externally and internally.

TYPE OF PLANT Lemon balm is a perennial whose leaves have a fresh, light, lemon fragrance. It's a small bush, spreading 1–2 feet and reaching 3 feet in height. The herb has very small white flowers from July through September. It repels insects but attracts honeybees. This plant is also known as balm or melissa.

HOW TO GROW Plant seeds in autumn or early spring. This is also the time to divide mature plants if desired. Propagate the herb from cuttings in the spring and summer. It self-seeds extensively and transplants easily. Put lemon balm in an area with full sun and well-drained or moist, sandy soil. It is prone to powdery mildew, so avoid overhead watering. Mulch the plant carefully during the winter to protect from frost.

HARVESTING Harvest leaves in midsummer, and spread on screens to dry. Alternatively, clip branches and hang to dry. To get the most healing properties from lemon balm, use it fresh.

PREPARATION AND DOSAGE Drink lemon balm tea as often as you like. Use a handful of crushed, fresh leaves for 1 teapot of hot water. You can add several drops of the volatile oil.

This is an herb that is best grown in your garden and prepared promptly. Lemon balm loses some of its essential oils unless carefully dried at about 90°F with circulating air for a couple of days, then promptly stored in a dark, air-tight container. Even then, use it within three months.

Its essential oil can be applied to herpes lesions, also called cold sores, when they erupt.

PRECAUTIONS There are no warnings or side effects reported for this herb. Lemon balm is safe even for infants, children, and older adults.

LICORICE, AN HERB with a sweet-tasting root, has a wealth of healing properties. It is antiviral, anti-inflammatory, and very mildly estrogenic and can be used as a laxative, expectorant, and liver booster. It also supports the adrenal glands.

HEALING PROPERTIES A potent antiviral, licorice fights off flu and other viruses as well as the herpes virus when applied directly to the sore.

It is a strong anti-inflammatory. Licorice is useful in soothing stomach or intestinal inflammation, rheumatoid arthritis's inflamed joints, inflamed airways in asthma conditions, and external skin inflammations. One of its anti-inflammatory compounds, glycyrrhizin, helps the body's natural cortisol, a steroid from the adrenal gland, to circulate throughout the body longer than normal. Cortisol itself reduces inflammation. Many prescription steroids, such as cortisone or prednisone, mimic the action of cortisol. However, these medications suppress immune function, often at a time when it is needed

to fight off infections. The good news is that licorice does not appear to suppress immunity and may even enhance immune function while still quelling inflammation. Both licorice, taken at high doses for long periods of time, and prescription medications do have similar side effects, however, including fluid retention, weight gain, and high blood pressure.

Japanese researchers have been using an injectable form of licorice for years to treat patients with hepatitis and AIDS. It is unknown if licorice taken orally would have similar benefits.

If you have low blood pressure, licorice may be helpful. A health professional should monitor your blood pressure while you're taking licorice. Many people with chronic fatigue syndrome have difficulties regulating their blood pressure, which tends to be low. Clinicians have suggested that licorice may help correct this problem.

Licorice is an excellent remedy for ulcers. It prompts mucosal cells in the stomach to secrete more protective mucus and improve the health of the stomach lining. It does not decrease stomach acid. Often a deglycyrrhizinated form of licorice is used to treat ulcers. It is just as effective and has none of the side effects mentioned above. In test tube studies, the flavonoids in deglycyrrhizinated licorice (DGL) have even been shown to kill *Helicobacter pylori,* the bacteria that causes most ulcers.

TYPE OF PLANT Licorice is a perennial that grows up to 3 feet tall. It is native to warm climates but can be grown in

temperate areas if moved indoors during the winter. Licorice produces a very deep taproot. The plant flowers in the summer, looking very much like other legumes, and if the growing season is long, it will produce a seed pod.

HOW TO GROW Sow seed in early spring or late fall. Cuttings can be taken from suckers. Place in well-drained, sandy soil in an area with full sun to partial shade. Licorice will tolerate only a light frost. This makes licorice a container-garden candidate so that it can be moved inside during winter.

HARVESTING Dig licorice roots in late fall or early winter. Be sure to leave enough root crowns to sprout the following year. Sometimes, however, cutting the root off will result in the crowns dying as well. Carefully wash licorice roots and place in a shady place to dry.

PREPARATION AND DOSAGE

Dried licorice roots can be chewed on and sometimes bring comfort to children who experience discomfort from cutting their permanent teeth. They can also be soothing to a sore throat. Make tea or tinctures from the root. Licorice can be consumed as tea, tincture, or syrup or in capsules. Limit licorice to 3 cups tea or ½–1 teaspoon tincture per day. DGL is available as chewable tablets. Mixing DGL with saliva before swallowing is important to ensure that it works, so don't use capsule

forms. Take 1–2 tablets before meals.

PRECAUTIONS

Licorice can elevate blood pressure. Do not use this herb if you have hypertension or are taking medication to reduce your blood pressure. If your blood pressure is normal, consuming licorice will probably not increase it.

Large doses, more than 5 cups per day, may cause bloating and fluid retention. Drinking 1 cup per day for several months can also bring on these symptoms.

Do not use licorice if you are pregnant.

Eat plenty of vegetables, especially dandelion greens in salads, while taking licorice as potassium helps offset potential side effects.

MARSHMALLOW

THIS SOFT, WOOLLY looking herb is a demulcent, soothing irritated or inflamed mucous membranes. It's even known for stimulating immune function by increasing the production and action of white blood cells.

HEALING PROPERTIES It's marshmallow's high mucilage content that gives it demulcent properties, helping it heal wounds and skin irritations as well as internal tissues. Marshmallow's demulcent actions and slight expectorant capabilities are also useful to the respiratory tract. Human studies show it relieves the discomfort of sore throats and coughs. To date, scientific studies have not been done to confirm the traditional wisdom about marshmallow's other healing abilities.

Taken internally, this herb is very calming to irritated areas in the mouth and the digestive tract. It soothes an irritated or inflamed stomach lining and may help heal ulcers. Other irritations along the intestinal tract also respond to marshmallow's subtle actions. Marshmallow has very mild laxative properties as well.

Bladder infections, especially chronic ones, may respond well to mallow preparations. The herb has slight diuretic activity and helps relieve inflammation of the urinary tract. It is often mixed with antibacterial herbs when used to treat bladder infections, sometimes eliminating the need for repeated courses of prescription antibiotics.

Used topically, a poultice of this herb may help heal cuts, abrasions, rashes, bruises, and insect bites. Applied warm, it draws out impurities and heals.

The white, puffy marshmallows in the store were named after this herb because its roots were originally made into a confection that had a similar texture to the current marshmallows.

TYPE OF PLANT Marshmallow is a 4–foot-tall perennial. It grows wild in the eastern United States in moist woodlands, saltwater marshes, or other damp areas, often near salt water. It has woolly stems and large, soft leaves and produces pinkish or pale blue flowers in mid-summer, starting in its second year. A hardy herb, marshmallow will tolerate hot, dry summers and cold winters.

HOW TO GROW In mild climates, start seeds in the fall. Take cuttings or divide the plant in the fall. Choose a place with full sun to partial shade and moist, light soil that is fairly rich.

HARVESTING Gather flowers while they are in bloom and seeds shortly thereafter, especially during the months of July and August. Leaves can be collected anytime.

Wait to collect taproots until the autumn of the second year. Clip rootlets that run laterally. Wash thoroughly; peel off the corklike bark, slice, then dry.

PREPARATION AND DOSAGE
Dried roots can be used to make teas, pills, or tinctures. Drink tea freely. Use 1 teaspoon to 1 tablespoon flower; fresh, crushed leaves; or dried root per 1 cup of water. To treat bladder infections, drink at least 3–4 cups per day mixed with other antibacterial herbs. Teas are better than tinctures for bladder infections, since it is always important to drink plenty of fluids when you have this condition. If using tincture, you may use up to 2 teaspoons per day.

Make a marshmallow poultice by mashing or blending fresh root with just enough water to make a thick gel. Apply directly to the skin.

PRECAUTION All mallows, including marshmallow, are considered safe and nontoxic and have no side effects.

MILK THISTLE

MILK THISTLE'S main claim to fame is its ability to support, detoxify, and nourish the liver. From cirrhosis to hepatitis and jaundice, milk thistle helps an ailing liver.

HEALING PROPERTIES The liver is one of the most complex and important organs of the body. It eventually processes or stores every nutrient you eat. Blood from the digestive tract goes straight to the liver, carrying with it a plethora of absorbed substances. The liver detoxifies compounds that can harm the body, makes bile that is needed to properly digest fat, and processes hormones that regulate body processes such as blood sugar levels.

Milk thistle is just the answer for the diligent and often overworked liver. This herb is rich in potent antioxidants, essential oils, and a group of flavonoids called silymarin. Compounds in milk thistle greatly increase glutathione levels in the body's cells. Glutathione is an antioxidant that detoxifies environmental pollutants and deactivates free radicals.

The flavonoids in milk thistle are able to repair damaged liver cells, offer protection to existing cells, and support the liver in making new cells. This herb is so effective that it has prevented death in people who accidentally consumed *Amanita*, a highly poisonous mushroom that normally causes liver failure and death.

Milk thistle has been shown specifically to decrease liver damage caused by long-term use of medications by people with serious mental health problems. It is likely, although not yet proved, that milk thistle could have the same effect for other medications.

Jaundice, hepatitis, cirrhosis, and liver enzyme tests typically improve after about two weeks of starting milk thistle therapy. Clinical trials have documented the efficacy of this herb so thoroughly that even mainstream journals are publishing articles by liver experts supporting its use.

It is traditionally used to improve mothers' milk. It is a close relative of artichokes, which also benefit the liver, but not as much as milk thistle does.

TYPE OF PLANT

Milk thistle grows easily as an annual or biennial. It often reaches 3 feet in height. Milk thistle is, as its name implies, a thistle, and the large, shiny leaves have white veins between the green, hence its name. The flower-bearing thistles that produce violet-blue flowers in late summer to early fall have spines as well. In the wild, this herb lives in moist, rocky areas or along roadsides.

HOW TO GROW

Often considered a weed, this thistle is not hard to grow. Plant seeds in the springtime in a place with well-drained soil and plenty of sunshine.

HARVESTING

Use the seeds, leaves, and shoots of this plant. Gather shoots and leaves in the spring. Wait for seeds to ripen in the summer.

PREPARATION AND DOSAGE

Leaves and shoots can be eaten raw in salad or steamed—just be sure to trim off the sharp outer edges before doing so.

Dry the seeds or make a tincture of them. Seeds can also be ground and sprinkled on food.

Use up to 3 cups per day of milk thistle tea or ½–1 teaspoon of tincture three times a day. This herb can also be consumed in capsule form—take 2 capsules two or three times per day.

To support the liver and help detoxify it, take milk thistle daily for several months.

PRECAUTIONS

Milk thistle is considered safe, and no toxicities or side effects are associated with it. High doses may have a mild laxative effect.

MULLEIN

MULLEIN IS particularly effective for disorders of the respiratory tract. It has demulcent and mild expectorant abilities. Used externally, this herb can soothe skin and brighten fair hair.

HEALING PROPERTIES Mullein contains mucilage, which helps ease irritated mucous membranes. Its saponins deliver expectorant activity, while its flavonoids help prevent inflammation and cell damage. These characteristics make mullein a good choice for treating hoarseness, tight coughs, whooping cough, bronchitis, and even asthma. Ayurvedic physicians also prescribe this herb for coughs. Historically, lung disorders were remedied by mullein. Although contemporary practitioners of all kinds find overwhelming clinical evidence of this herb's benefits, there have been no human studies of it in modern times.

The flowers and leaves of this plant can come to the aid of the digestive tract. Their compounds may be useful for treating colitis. The urinary tract benefits, too. Mullein is a mild diuretic and decreases inflammation of the urinary system.

Mullein's flowers are reputed to be a mild sedative and helpful for those suffering from insomnia. Flower infusions can be added to creams and to shampoos to brighten the hair.

Externally, boils and sores may be successfully treated with a mullein poultice. Crushed flowers infused into olive oil and sometimes including garlic make eardrops that may reduce the pain and inflammation of an earache. Consult a health care practitioner first to be sure rupture hasn't occurred. Do not use if the eardrum is known to be ruptured.

TYPE OF PLANT Mullein is a biennial plant whose yellow flower stalk can reach up to 7 feet tall. This plant likes rocky soil, and its woolly leaves are covered with soft, fine hairs. It is unusually soft for a plant. But what is soft to us is self-defense for this dry-climate herb. Animals avoid eating the leaves because the tiny hairs are irritating to their mucous membranes. These hairs also help the plant hold in moisture and repel insects.

Typically considered a weed, mullein often grows along roadsides or in fallow fields.

HOW TO GROW Sow seeds in spring or summer; this herb easily self-seeds. Mullein will tolerate any type of soil—rich, poor, rocky, or dry. It does best in full sun.

HARVESTING Use the flowers and leaves of this herb. Harvest leaves during the first year of growth. The flower stalk appears in the second year; collect flowers as soon as they open.

PREPARATION AND DOSAGE To prepare mullein flowers, remove the green portions and gently dry the rest of the flower or pluck out the yellow florets that continue to appear throughout August. Let them dry naturally, without added heat, to preserve the yellow color, which contains healing substances. Dry the leaves, too.

Mullein can be taken in tea, tincture, or capsule form. Drink up to 3 cups of tea or 1 teaspoon of tincture per day. When making tea, strain the liquid through a fine cloth to remove tiny hairs that may irritate the throat.

PRECAUTIONS Mullein does not appear to have side effects. The only precaution is related to the fine hairs that may cause irritation either internally or externally in sensitive people. It may cause a skin rash in some people.

Do not use mullein oil in the ear if the eardrum has ruptured.

NASTURTIUM

ALL YOU HAVE to do is eat these colorful flowers and attractive leaves to benefit from their medicinal properties. Their lively, peppery taste can spark up many summer dishes. They have been used to treat such maladies as bronchitis and urinary tract infections. Nasturtium has unusual antibiotic properties.

HEALING PROPERTIES Unlike most antibiotics, this herb reportedly does not kill off the "friendly" or good bacteria that live in the intestinal tract. This friendly bacteria is beneficial to colon health, helping to keep the harmful bacteria in check. The harmful bacteria make toxins that irritate the colon wall and may ultimately lead to cancerous lesions. During a normal course of antibiotics, the good bacteria are killed off along with the infectious bacteria the drug was fighting. This gives harmful bacteria a chance to take over, so it is always a good idea to reestablish the friendly bacteria after taking antibiotics. Use such products as probiotic supplements or yogurts whose labels list live acidophilus and bifidus cultures.

Nasturtium itself holds promise as an antibiotic. Researchers believe that the natural compounds in this plant may be effective in fighting certain bacteria that have developed a resistance to antibiotic drugs.

When consumed, the leaves and flowers of this plant help to fight lung infections and bronchitis. It has also been shown to be effective against urinary tract infections and infections of the reproductive organs.

Externally, nasturtium may relieve itchy skin. Rub a little of the fresh plant juice directly on the skin or make a poultice or compress and apply it to the affected area.

TYPE OF PLANT These colorful annuals come in several varieties that either produce a small,

1-foot–tall bush or a rambling vine. The flowers range in color from light yellow to orange, burgundy, gold, and even pink. The rich-green leaves are circular in shape. Nasturtiums are easy to grow, make a showy plant in the garden, and are often useful for companion planting. They are known to repel certain pests. Choose vine varieties for hanging planters, window boxes, or trellises.

HOW TO GROW The large nasturtium seeds can be placed in the ground in late spring. They are easy-to-grow plants, tolerant of many conditions. They do well in sun or partial shade and in average or poor, moist soil.

HARVESTING Fresh leaves and flowers can be picked anytime, as needed. Collect unripe seeds for pickling.

PREPARATION AND DOSAGE Nasturtiums can be made into an infusion or tincture, although they are most often eaten fresh. Infuse flowers or seeds in vinegar for use on salads. The buds can also be pickled in vinegar and used as substitutes for capers. Remove individual petals and add to fresh vegetable dishes or salads to lend a peppery flavor and beautiful colors.

Nasturtiums nicely complement a fresh corn relish. Include them in sandwiches for an unusual taste treat. Flowers can be stuffed with herbed cream cheese. Use leaves as a fresh green to spark up and freshen the taste of a tossed salad.

PRECAUTIONS The seeds, if eaten in large quantities, act as a strong laxative.

NETTLE

FORGIVE THE INNOCENT NETTLE. It packs a nasty sting but is rich in minerals and healing abilities. Nettle is very versatile, treating such conditions as kidney and bladder problems, gout, malnutrition, anemia, diarrhea, hayfever, and eczema. Quite a lineup for an herb you don't really want to touch.

HEALING PROPERTIES Nettle is a great addition to a meal, providing absorbable sources of iron, calcium, phosphorus, and magnesium as well as vitamins A and C. Because of its high mineral content, nettle has a reputation for treating anemia and malnutrition. It has a high amount of protein for a plant.

This unusual herb also contains anti-inflammatory flavonoids. This makes it useful for treating skin conditions such as eczema and rashes as well as keeping blood vessels in good shape. Capsules of freeze-dried nettle were shown in a modern study to alleviate hay fever, presumably because of their anti-inflammatory activity.

Its diuretic properties aid bladder problems and reduce edema, the collection of fluids in tissues. However, the most clearly proved action of nettle in the urinary tract is in reducing an enlarged prostate, alone or in combination with the herb saw palmetto. The leaves and root have been shown in numerous studies to shrink an enlarged prostate gland. However, the root appears to be more effective in this specific application.

Two controlled human studies have documented the effectiveness of nettle for treating patients with rheumatoid arthritis. Historically, fresh nettles were slapped on inflamed joints, and the pain of the nettles soon subsided and seemed to take the arthritis away with it, at least temporarily. Now it seems internal use of capsules or tinctures are effective, either alone or contributing to the benefit of uncomfortable external applications.

Gout is not nearly as common as it used to be but does occur occasionally. It is a disorder in which crystals of uric acid collect in joints and tissues, resulting in painful inflammation. Traditional folk medicine recommends several tablespoons of fresh nettle juice per day to help remove uric acid from these areas, decreasing the pain.

This herb has the ability to lower blood sugar levels slightly and to diminish profuse menstruation.

As a hair conditioner, nettle provides shine, and it has been used traditionally to prevent hair loss, although this has never been investigated scientifically.

TYPE OF PLANT This perennial plant grows abundantly along damp paths and roadways. It reaches from 3 to 6 feet in height. Thousands of tiny "hairs" on its leaves contain formic acid, which stings the skin upon contact.

HOW TO GROW Nettle can be grown from divided plants or from seeds sown in the spring. It likes rich, moist soil with full sun to partial shade. This herb is very invasive, and you will need to aggressively cut it back more than once each summer and before it goes to seed. Nettle attracts beneficial insects.

HARVESTING Use the roots and leaves of the nettle plant. Be sure to wear thick gardening-type gloves when handling to avoid the stinging formic acid.

Drying, cooking, or grinding nettle eliminates its sting.

Use dried or fresh nettle in tea or tinctures. Drink up to 2 cups tea per day or 1–3 teaspoons tincture.

Nettle can be juiced; limit intake to 2 ounces per day. You may prefer to mix nettle with other vegetable juices to make a more appealing flavor.

Nettle can be used as a leafy green vegetable—the leaves lose their sting when cooked. Steam lightly and serve as you would kale or spinach. Nettle may also be added to soups, casseroles, and pasta dishes.

To make hair conditioner, simmer a large handful of nettles in an enamel saucepan for 15 minutes, or grind and cover with vinegar, shaking daily for two weeks. Strain, cool, and refrigerate.

PRECAUTIONS Always wear thick gloves when you are handling nettles.

Rarely there are reports of allergic reactions to nettle, characterized by dizziness and fainting. Consuming large amounts of leaves from older plants may irritate the kidneys, so always use young spring leaves.

Topical applications of fresh nettles can be a useful treatment for aching joints, but do not attempt this unless you are under the supervision of an herbal expert.

OAT BRAN IS WELL-KNOWN and well-researched for its ability to lower blood cholesterol levels. But oats are also good at healing wounds and skin irritations when used topically. They are even used as a nerve tonic.

HEALING PROPERTIES Oatmeal baths and poultices stop the itching of chicken pox and rashes. They soothe dry, flaky skin and serve as a gentle but effective facial scrub. They encourage wounds to heal.

Oats contain gramine, a phyto-chemical that has gentle seda-tive proper-ties. B vitamins also contribute to its nerve tonic effects. Researchers note that fresh oats help in the treat-ment of drug and nicotine addictions, reducing cravings and apprehension in prelimi-nary studies.

Oats are renowned for their soluble fiber content, which binds onto cholesterol and prevents its absorption. But oats also have insoluble fiber, which keeps the large intestine running smoothly and can help prevent colon and rectal cancers.

Tea made from oat straw gives you a boost of healthful minerals.

TYPE OF PLANT Oats need to be replanted annually. They are a grass that grows 2–4 feet in height. The stem is hollow with flat, skinny leaves. A "hairy" cluster at the top of the stalk hides the grooved grains.

HOW TO GROW Sow oat seeds in the spring. Oats prefer full sun.

HARVESTING Use the fresh, unripe seed; the ripe seed called an oat berry or oat groat; and the shaft, known as the oat straw. Gather oat straw and fresh oats in the green, milky stage during spring, but wait until late summer to harvest the oat berry, which has ripened and dried by that time.

PREPARATION AND DOSAGE You can dry oat straw and oat groats to make a tincture. Do not dry the fresh oat seed, or it will lose some of its healing properties. Instead, make a fresh tincture of it. Limit intake of tinctures to 4 teaspoons per day.

Oatmeal and oat bran cereal are common ways to get the health benefits of oats. Either cook it hot in the morning or soak steel-cut oats in milk the night before and set them in the refrigerator. Oat groats can be ground into flour to make a partial substitute for wheat flour.

It's best not to use rolled oats for cooking because they are heated in order to be rolled, and that process destroys much of the B vitamins. When oat groats are cut with steel mills, heat is not used and so these nutrients are retained. Steel-cut oats are also called Irish or Scottish oats.

For tea, use 1 tablespoon oats or oat straw per cup of hot water. Drink several cups per day.

For the bath, tie oats along with other herbs in a piece of porous fabric or old nylon stocking and place over the faucet while hot water is running. To make a poultice, grind oats in a coffee grinder or food processor, then add water and stir to make a paste.

PRECAUTIONS Oats contain a glutenlike protein (though less than wheat, barley, or rye), so if you are sensitive to gluten or have celiac disease, avoid them in food or medicine. However, some studies show that many people with celiac disease can eat oats without any problem. Consult a health care professional who has nutritional knowledge.

If you quickly increase intake of any fiber-rich food, including oats, you may experience discomfort. Always remember to increase fluid intake when increasing fiber to avoid blockage and constipation.

COMPOUNDS IN THE ROOTS of Oregon grape have been investigated in the laboratory, verifying that it is able to kill certain bacteria, viruses, and even yeast.

HEALING PROPERTIES Oregon grape contains berberine, an antimicrobial. It kills microbes such as *Giardia, E. coli,* and other intestinal parasites as well as the yeast *Candida.* Oregon grape root, then, can help treat diarrhea and infections of the digestive tract as well as vaginal yeast infections, colds, and flu. Made into a decoction, this herb makes a good eyewash for conjunctivitis or a skin wash for infected wounds. The tincture can be applied directly to an area with herpes or a canker sore, but the alcohol may sting. If the discomfort is pronounced, use a decocted tea.

Most of the research on Oregon grape has been on its topical use for treating psoriasis. Creams made from Oregon grape effectively relieve psoriasis in many people. It may also help other chronic skin diseases such as eczema.

As a bitter herb, Oregon grape root stimulates digestive juices and bile production. It also tones the intestinal tract and is used for general gastrointestinal problems.

Berberine improves blood flow, especially to the liver. Oregon grape is used to treat liver ailments such as jaundice and hepatitis and shows promise even with cirrhosis.

The berries are high in vitamin C and, because of their dark purple color, are probably rich in flavonoids. Flavonoids protect and improve the integrity of blood vessels and capillaries, promoting the health of the heart and circulatory system. Little research has been conducted on the berries.

TYPE OF PLANT Oregon grape is a hardy, leafy, evergreen shrub. It reaches 3–6 feet in height and spreads to about 4 feet, or over vast areas in the moist Northwest. Its leaves are prickly and turn crimson in the fall. In the spring, the plant awakens with clusters of tiny yellow flowers and produces small, dark purple berries. In the wild, it grows in coniferous forests.

HOW TO GROW Plant seeds in spring. Take cuttings in late spring to summer, get them started, then set them out the following spring. This herb produces rhizomes, lateral rootlike stems with shoots. Plant in an area that has well-drained, rich soil in full sun to partial shade. Oregon grape is suitable for a container garden.

HARVESTING Harvest berries in the fall. Also dig roots in the fall, then dry in a paper bag.

PREPARATION AND DOSAGE The most medicinal portion of the roots is the yellow material beneath the outer root bark. To get the most benefit from it, you can use the whole root to make tea or tincture. However, peeling the inner bark off the root will make it stronger. Drink 3–6 cups of tea or use ½ teaspoon tincture every 30 minutes to fight off an oncoming illness. Reduce dosages over the next several days. If you are using capsules, take 1 or 2 several times a day.

Oregon grape berries may be eaten raw, made into jam, or added to soups.

PRECAUTIONS Do not use this herb if you are pregnant.

Eyewash made of this herb must be greatly diluted and sterile.

Do not treat serious gastrointestinal infections such as giardia without professional medical help. If diarrhea lasts more than two to three days despite Oregon grape treatment, see your doctor.

PASSION FLOWER

THIS COLORFUL and intricate flower is said to reveal the story of Christ's crucifixion. The lush and tropical-looking vine has a reputation as a sedative and tranquilizer without being addictive.

HEALING PROPERTIES Flower components of this herb are used in prescription medications throughout Europe. It is effective at relieving anxiety, restlessness, stress, insomnia, and nervous disorders in general. Some have even used it to treat epilepsy and hyperactivity. In Europe it is also prescribed for general tension and fatigue.

Passion flower's antispasmodic properties relieve muscle tension, although it is not a strong pain reliever. This may make the herb helpful for reducing high blood pressure, as it may relax the muscles that line artery walls. It has been used to treat heart palpitations as well.

Passion flower contains flavonoids, which promote the health of the heart and arteries, helping them remain elastic. It is these flavonoids, along with substances called alkaloids, that give this herb its tranquilizing qualities. Although these flavonoids bind to the same receptor in the brain as drugs such as Valium, passion flower has never been shown to be addictive or have other side effects.

Numerous animal investigations have confirmed the activity of passion flower, but human studies are lacking.

TYPE OF PLANT This creeping vine is a perennial. It produces complex flowers with several shades of white, lavender, and pink in each flower. The leaves are a contrasting green with three, four, or five lobes. Coiling tendrils make it an excellent climber. The plant produces small yellow berries.

HOW TO GROW Passion flower likes a lot of sun along with occasional shade. It prefers deep soil that's not too rich in fertilizer, or else foliage develops rather than flowers. Replace the topsoil around the base of the vine each spring. Trim old branches in later winter or early spring to encourage blooming. This flowering vine can be grown indoors if you have a large container for it, but it won't reach its normal height of 25—30 feet. Passion flower is susceptible to certain pests, so keep a protective eye on it.

HARVESTING Harvest the vine at the end of flowering if you want to include flowers or after the flowers are done blooming for just the tips of the vine.

PREPARATION AND DOSAGE Dry the flowers or make tea or tincture of them. Take up to 4 cups of tea per day during times of severe stress; reduce the dosage as symptoms improve. Take ½ teaspoon of tincture two to eight times per day for anxiety. Start with the smallest dose to which you respond, increasing only if needed and then only for short periods of time. Tinctures taken in this manner can also help relieve muscle tension. Two capsules can be taken several times a day. To help you fall asleep, take 2 or 3 capsules one hour before bedtime.

PRECAUTION Passion flower has a blue-colored cousin that is considerably hardier and often grown in cooler areas. However, the blue passion flower plant should not be used medicinally.

Start with small doses and increase gradually to see how your body responds. Take as low a dose as possible to prevent mental fogginess. Taking too much over a long period of time can depress the nervous system.

When used in moderation, passion flower is considered safe.

PEPPERMINT

THIS COMMON HERB has many culinary, medicinal, and aromatherapy uses. Its carminative properties dispel gas in the intestines. Its antispasmodic abilities ease stomach cramps and colon spasms. Its icy warmth helps soothe sore muscles. It gives a delightful flavor to foods and beverages, and its aroma lifts the spirits.

HEALING PROPERTIES Menthol, peppermint's main essential oil, is responsible for many of its therapeutic properties. Ideal for soothing an upset stomach and irritable bowel syndrome, counteracting too much stomach acid, and relieving intestinal cramps, peppermint is even safe and effective for a baby with colic. It is believed to act primarily as an antispasmodic. Several clinical studies have confirmed the efficacy of peppermint for many of these conditions.

Concentrated extracts of the oil have been shown to help dissolve gallstones in some people. Do not attempt to treat gallstones by yourself, as there may be serious complications. However, along with dandelion root, this herb may prevent stones.

Used topically, peppermint reduces pain, burning, and inflammation. It can temporarily stop itching, including that arising from insect bites and eczema.

It is a potent decongestant and can relieve headaches. It has only mild antimicrobial abilities, so it is rarely used to kill bacteria, fungi, and viruses.

Studies looking into aromatherapy uses of peppermint determined that inhaling this herb's fragrance stimulated brain waves, increased concentration, and helped people stay awake. Aromatherapists have long used mint to decrease mental fatigue, to increase memory, and to lift the spirits.

TYPE OF PLANT Mint is an easy-to-grow perennial that comes in many varieties: Peppermint and spearmint are just two of them. It's a low-growing herb, reaching 2 feet in height but spreading easily with underground stems. Mint flowers in mid-summer. It has a reputation for repelling insects such as aphids, cabbage pests, and flies.

HOW TO GROW Divide mint plants anytime during the growing season or take cuttings in midsummer. Give them a place with full sun to partial shade and moist soil. Because of mint's invasive and spreading nature, you may prefer to keep it in containers or sunken pots in the garden.

HARVESTING Harvest leaves anytime. New shoots are best picked just as the plant begins to flower, in midsummer. Hang to dry or freeze.

PREPARATION AND DOSAGE In the kitchen, use mint in jellies, salads, and sauces and to flavor vegetable dishes.

Make tea or tinctures from mint leaves; use freely. Leaves can be either fresh or dried. Limit tea to 3 cups per day. For a baby with colic, give 1 teaspoon of tea or place a cloth soaked in peppermint tea on the baby's tummy.

Essential oil, as long as it is diluted in a carrier oil, can be rubbed directly onto skin surfaces and is easily absorbed. Use 1–3 drops per ¼ cup carrier oil or until you notice a light fragrance. For decongestant purposes, put several drops in a bowl of hot water and inhale the steam. Close your eyes so the volatile fumes do not burn them.

Put drops of essential oil in an aroma lamp in your office or study, or add it to sachets or potpourri.

Used internally or externally, mint is safe for pregnant women.

Capsules of enteric-coated peppermint oil appear to be most useful for irritable bowel syndrome, according to studies. Take 1–2 capsules three times per day.

PRECAUTIONS Peppermint may relax the tight muscle at the bottom of the esophagus, the esophageal sphincter, which keeps stomach acid and stomach contents from coming up towards the throat. If used excessively, its essential oils along with the uprising stomach acid may damage the tender tissues in this area. Therefore, if you have any problems of the esophagus such as hiatal hernia, gastroesophageal reflux disease (GERD), or chronic heartburn, use mint sparingly. Peppermint can actually worsen such conditions.

Rarely, people are allergic to mint, experiencing headaches, stomach upset, or a rash.

People with the genetic condition glucose-6-phosphate dehydrogenase deficiency should avoid internal use of the essential oil.

RED CLOVER

RESEARCHERS ARE INVESTIGATING whether clover, because of its biochanin A content, might be able to prevent and treat cancerous tumors. The herb's antioxidants and its ability to stimulate the immune system enhance its promise as an anticancer agent.

HEALING PROPERTIES Due to its resin content, red clover is one possible treatment for respiratory congestion and coughs. It helps rid the body of excess mucus.

Coumarin is another phytochemical in red clover. Coumarin tones the veins and has been shown in controlled studies to help people with chronic venous insufficiency. It also appears to be a diuretic, and studies show it will help relieve edema. There is even preliminary evidence that it fights melanoma in humans.

Red clover also possesses phytoestrogens. These are plant estrogens that are able to mimic the body's own estrogen to a very small degree. This is a good thing during times of low estrogen, such as after menopause. Researchers believe that phytoestrogens may contribute to the prevention of heart disease and osteoporosis in postmenopausal women without increasing their risk of estrogen-related cancers. These same substances are being tested to determine how they might affect younger, premenopausal women. The theory is that the phytoestrogens might displace the body's own more potent estrogen, thereby diminishing the risk of breast, uterine, and other hormone-related cancers. However, this is still under investigation, and the results may show that there is an increased risk. Traditionally, this herb was used to treat infertility and chronic miscarriage, both of which could be related to the plant's phytoestrogen content. At least one published case study has suggested that clover extracts may help men with prostate cancer.

Red clover has anti-inflammatory properties and is recommended for skin conditions such as eczema and psoriasis.

TYPE OF PLANT Red clover is a perennial legume, adding nitrogen to the soil as it grows. Its leaves are in groups of three—unless you're lucky enough to find a four-leafed one. Clover is often used as a cover crop to increase the soil's nitrogen content. However, it produces runners that spread easily; the plant and runners must be chopped very well when tilling in the cover crop or you'll end up with clover all over the garden. This fragrant herb attracts honeybees.

HOW TO GROW Sow seeds in spring or fall. It likes full sun and moist, well-drained soil.

HARVESTING Gather flowers and young leaves while the plant is in bloom.

PREPARATION AND DOSAGE Use red clover's flowers in summer salads; add its florets to herbal iced tea. Its leaves do not digest well raw, so cook them or use them dried or for tea. Take up to 3 cups hot or iced tea per day.

PRECAUTIONS Because of red clover's estrogenic effects, do not use it if you have uterine fibroids or an increased risk for estrogen-related cancers. Again, this is purely theoretical and clover may actually be helpful for these conditions.

Clover occasionally causes digestive gas.

Do not use moldy or fermented clover, as it may contain blood-thinning compounds not found in the fresh herb.

RED RASPBERRY

RED RASPBERRY LEAVES have long been used to prepare mothers-to-be for childbirth. The substances in this herb boast astringent, stimulant, and toning abilities. In addition, raspberry is often used to alleviate digestive upsets, such as nausea, vomiting, diarrhea, and morning sickness.

HEALING PROPERTIES Indeed, red raspberry is known as one of the "woman's herbs." It not only may help calm morning sickness but can also help prevent miscarriage and reduce the pain of labor. Raspberry leaves accomplish this by toning the muscles of the uterus and pelvis, especially when taken daily for the last three months of pregnancy. As yet, scientific studies are lacking to support the efficacy of red raspberry for any of the uses midwives have long known to be true.

If used over a period of time, red raspberry leaves also diminish menstrual cramps or excessive menstrual bleeding.

Women find that red raspberry can help with other problems of the uterus, such as endometriosis and fibroids.

Raspberry is so mild even children can use it. It is sometimes recommended along with other treatments for children who are suffering a bout of diarrhea.

This herb's astringent qualities make it an effective skin treatment. Irritated skin, sores, or open wounds can be soothed by a gentle wash of raspberry leaf infusion. It also makes a good gargle or mouthwash.

Historically this herb was prescribed for additional ailments such as ulcers, mouth sores, and hemorrhoids. Whether research proves it is useful for these conditions remains to be seen. Because it is a mild herb without side effects, you may wish to experiment with it yourself for these conditions. However, if you have an ulcer, first seek the help of a doctor knowledgeable about herbs.

TYPE OF PLANT The raspberry is a bramble bush with thorny stems. It reaches 4 feet or more in height with a spread of at least 3 feet. Typically it's hard to tell where one bush ends and another begins. It sends out shoots or canes that, when they touch the ground, take root and start a new plant. Its leaves have saw-toothed edges and are green on top and grayish-white on the underside. It produces white flowers that give way to raspberries, which ripen in early summer, typically June and July. The varieties *Rubus idaeus* and *Rubus strigosus* are preferred for their medicinal value. Many other varieties are cultivated for their fruit.

HOW TO GROW Raspberry bushes like rich, well-drained soil and full sun. To propagate, divide roots or take ½-inch cuttings and plant them in several inches of soil. Raspberry grows easily and spreads rapidly; be careful where you put it.

HARVESTING Leaves can be gathered anytime, but preferably before the berries start to appear. Harvest berries when they separate from their branchlet with a very slight tug.

PREPARATION AND DOSAGE Make tea or tincture from the leaves. Even pregnant women can drink the flavorful tea freely. If using tincture, take up to ½ teaspoon three times per day.

Prepare raspberry tea to use as an external wash.

Red raspberries can be eaten fresh. See the profile on berries for serving suggestions and health benefits.

PRECAUTION Raspberry leaf tea has no known side effects and is considered safe for everyone, including children.

ROSEMARY

ROSEMARY IS PACKED with an abundance of healing and beneficial properties. Uses reach far beyond its popularity in the kitchen—from fighting cancer and aiding digestion to improving concentration and memory when smelling its essential oils.

HEALING PROPERTIES Rosemary's fragrance is so effective at improving concentration that you might consider using it in an aroma lamp for a child who has trouble concentrating on homework. Additionally, this herb strengthens the nervous system, helps keep emotions in check, and helps prevent mood swings. It is useful in stressful situations and for clearing the head, although scientific research has not been done to confirm rosemary's memory-enhancing effects.

Rosemary helps with headaches, too, which are relieved either by taking an infusion or applying diluted essential oil externally.

This herb is undergoing studies to determine its usefulness as an anticancer agent. It's full of antioxidants, flavonoids, and other phytochemicals. Diosmin, one of its flavonoids, strengthens blood vessels, improves circulation, and has successfully treated varicose veins. A footbath with rosemary helps cold or numb feet—indications of poor circulation. A liniment made with rosemary can be used to treat muscle spasms and rheumatism.

Because of its antiseptic properties, an infusion of this herb used as a gargle or a wash helps ease sore throats, gum infections, canker sores, eczema, and wounds.

Rosemary stimulates digestion by prompting the gallbladder to deliver bile for fat breakdown, and it reduces intestinal gas. Rosmanicine, a compound in rosemary, affects the smooth muscles of the intestines, helping them to keep moving.

This herb can inhibit kidney stone formation and help the liver carry out its detoxification duties. It also acts as an expectorant and diaphoretic. Rosemary even has a reputation as a hair tonic. Used in shampoo or conditioner, it can minimize dandruff and brighten dull, lifeless hair.

TYPE OF PLANT This pretty herb can be kept small and trimmed into a hedge or let loose to grow into a 4–6-foot shrub. It is an ideal container plant. Rosemary has evergreen, needle-shaped leaves that are green in color. It has pale blue flowers during the spring months.

HOW TO GROW Sow rosemary seeds, cuttings, or transplants in the spring. It prefers full sun but will tolerate partial shade. Plant it in sandy, alkaline soil. In colder climates, grow it in a pot so it can be moved to shelter in freezing weather. It needs protection from winter winds.

HARVESTING Pick rosemary leaves at any time and use them fresh. Cut small branches about 3–4 inches in length, without making the plant so short as to be unsightly or risk future growth, and hang to dry.

PREPARATION AND DOSAGE Rosemary leaves may be used fresh or dried for seasoning. Add tea, tincture, or oil to body lotions, massage oils, salves, and shampoos. For aromatherapy purposes, try combining it with a sweet herb to take the edge off its pungent aroma.

Make an infusion out of fresh leaves. Combine with other herbs, if desired, to use for sipping.

PRECAUTIONS Do not take undiluted rosemary oil internally; use with caution on skin. There are no reported side effects.

ST. JOHN'S WORT IS RICH in flavonoids, hypericin, pseudo-hypericin, and phloroglucinols with antiviral and antibacterial actions. It can ease the inflammation of such conditions as sprains, hemorrhoids, and varicose veins. Many people use it to counteract depression.

HEALING PROPERTIES Although numerous clinical trials proved that St. John's wort is an effective treatment for anxiety and depression, just how it works has not been confirmed. However, researchers believe it may be due in part to one of the plant's phytochemicals, hypericin. Studies suggest it may alter serotonin levels or receptor function, improving mood. Several studies reveal that after taking a standardized extract of this plant, feelings of depression, anxiety, and worthlessness improve significantly. It also enriches sleep quality in depressed persons, relieving both insomnia and excessive sleeping. Another study has shown it can help people suffering from seasonal affective disorder (SAD).

Tannins and oils in St. John's wort have antibacterial properties, and the herb is being investigated for its antiviral effects against the HIV virus. The National Cancer Institute is researching compounds in this herb to determine potential cancer-fighting ability. Early studies suggest it may be particularly helpful to those with brain cancer. This plant has also been used to treat skin and nerve problems, and it may be effective against nerve destruction.

TYPE OF PLANT St. John's wort is an erect and hardy perennial. It has bright yellow flowers during June and July, with flower stalks reaching 3 feet in height. Its green leaves are small and oblong, appearing to have pores when held up to the light. This plant grows naturally throughout North America in woodlands and meadows.

HOW TO GROW Sow seeds in the spring or transplant it from the wild; it moves easily. St. John's wort thrives in most soil and light conditions; it is very easy to grow.

HARVESTING This herb is best used fresh, so harvest only as much as you need at one time. The flowers and leaves should be taken after the plant has bloomed. The flowers will stain your hands reddish-purple.

PREPARATION AND DOSAGE Make infusions and tinctures while the plant is fresh. When dried, it loses many of its medicinal properties. It can be stored in oil in a dark container for up to two years.

To make the oil, soak clean, puréed leaves and flowers in olive oil. Set in a warm, light place for four to six weeks. Strain. Use externally only.

Tinctures can be taken in amounts of up to 1 teaspoon three times per day.

If you purchase St. John's wort products, choose those that are made either from the fresh plant or are freeze-dried.

PRECAUTIONS Do not take St. John's wort if you also take monoamine oxidase (MAO) inhibitors, although only a few cases of problems have been reported. Consuming large quantities can cause a skin rash after sun exposure. Originally classified as unsafe by the FDA, recent studies among AIDS patients with depression indicate that this herb is largely nontoxic when taken at recommended doses. To be safe, do not use for prolonged periods of time. Tell your doctor before taking this herb, and do not stop taking prescription antidepressants unless your doctor so advises.

SKULLCAP

SKULLCAP USUALLY GROWS like a weed throughout most of the world, and scientists are looking into its beneficial qualities. In Japan, studies reveal that skullcap may increase blood levels of "good" HDL cholesterol, helping to reduce atherosclerosis. In Russia, researchers have found the herb helps diminish stress-related heart disease.

HEALING PROPERTIES In China, the roots of a variety of skullcap called *Scutellaria baicalensis* (or *huang yin* in Chinese) support the liver and treat hepatitis, as well as reduce swelling. It is a strong anti-inflammatory. It inhibits the release of two substances, acetylcholine and histamine, which cause inflammation or allergylike symptoms. Taken internally, this herb can reduce inflammation and associated pain and swelling.

Scutellaria lateriflora, a variety of skullcap often found in the United States, is a useful sedative. It is helpful for gently calming nervous twitches and for general nervousness, including nervous headaches, anxiety, depression, and insomnia. It brings sleep to a troubled person without being strongly sedating. It has sometimes been used to treat epilepsy.

This herb also eases muscle tension and spasms, aiding relaxation. Its ability to soothe smooth muscles, including those that line arteries, may help to reduce high blood pressure.

As a slightly bitter herb, skullcap stimulates digestion and enhances the secretion of digestive juices.

Skullcap's flavonoid content supports immune function as well as heart and blood vessel health

TYPE OF PLANT Skullcap is a small perennial, reaching just 2 feet in height and 8 inches in diameter. It grows tall and slender, producing square-stemmed branches with opposite leaves. Its green leaves are slightly saw-toothed around their edges. During late spring and early summer, skullcap produces a bluish-purple flower comprised of two sections, or "lips." The herb got its name from the flowers, as they resemble the skullcaps worn in medieval times. In some regions it is called helmet flower, due to the flower's shape, or mad dog weed, because it was once used to treat rabies. The variety *Scutellaria lateriflora* is the one most commonly found in the eastern United States and southern Canada.

HOW TO GROW Sow skullcap seeds in the spring or divide its roots. This herb likes well-drained, moist soil with partial shade.

HARVESTING The leaves and flowers are the therapeutic portions of this plant. Collect skullcap leaves after the flowers have begun to bloom in the summer. Collect blooms after they have opened.

PREPARATION AND DOSAGE Dry the leaves and flowers for tea, tincture, or powders. To make capsules, crush dried leaves and fill gelatin capsules; use within a couple of months.

If using as a tea, you may wish to add mint or some other herb to tone down skullcap's slightly bitter flavor. Use 1 tablespoon of skullcap per cup of hot water and steep for 15 minutes. Use 2–3 cups of tea or ½ teaspoon tincture two to three times per day. If taking in capsule form, swallow 2 capsules every eight to twelve hours.

PRECAUTIONS There are no precautions or side effects for skullcap used in moderation.

Uva Ursi

THIS HERB IS FAMOUS for successfully treating problems of the urinary tract, especially bladder infections. For years, women in particular have turned to uva ursi for relief from urinary tract infections.

HEALING PROPERTIES This herb is loaded with astringent and antiseptic properties, thanks to substances called tannins and arbutin. In the body, arbutin is converted to a compound called hydroquinone, which is a urinary disinfectant. It is often recommended to treat illnesses caused by *Escherichia coli* (*E. coli*) and other organisms. Certain yeasts, such as *Candida*, may also succumb to the chemical compounds in uva ursi.

This small herb may relieve pelvic pain, too, especially when it is associated with urinary tract infections. It is often recommended for symptoms such as pelvic cramping accompanied by a heavy feeling.

Get an extra herbal punch by mixing uva ursi with other herbs that are helpful to the urinary tract, such as fennel and marshmallow.

TYPE OF PLANT Uva ursi is a perennial evergreen ground cover. It has thick, leathery-looking leaves. From the barest onset of spring, it produces white flowers that have a red tinge to them. Red berries follow the flowers. Uva ursi grows throughout the United States. It goes by many names including bearberry, beargrape, hogberry, rockberry, and mountain cranberry.

HOW TO GROW Start uva ursi from seeds or cuttings in the spring. Plants can be purchased from larger nurseries. This herb prefers rocky, dry soil with full sun. Once established, uva ursi takes care of itself; just make sure it gets water. Diseases and pests don't bother this plant.

HARVESTING Use the young leaves of uva ursi for medicinal purposes. Gather them in spring or early summer to avoid the high tannin levels that accumulate by autumn. Older leaves gathered late in the season can contain up to 40 percent tannins.

PREPARATION AND DOSAGE Dry leaves for infusions or tinctures. To benefit from uva ursi's healing properties, make a decoction: Boil the leaves in water to extract the arbutin compound. Use 1 tablespoon leaves per 2 cups of water; simmer, covered, for 10 to 15 minutes, then steep for an additional 20 minutes. Use this water as tea, consuming up to 3 cups per day.

Soaking the herb in cold water for 12 to 24 hours before using reduces tannin levels.

If using a tincture, take up to 1 teaspoon several times per day.

PRECAUTIONS Do not use uva ursi if you are pregnant, as it may stimulate the uterus and cause miscarriage or premature delivery. Avoid giving to children, as its effects may be too strong. This herb may rarely cause kidney irritation, so do not use it if you have a kidney disorder unless instructed to do so by a qualified health care provider. Use uva ursi only for a short duration to avoid stomach irritation due to the tannins and to avoid potentially hazardous accumulation of hydroquinone. Used short term for normal medicinal uses, this herb is considered perfectly safe.

Large amounts (1.5 ounces or more) of the dried leaves have been reported to poison people who are sensitive to uva ursi.

If you're experiencing blood in the urine or burning urination with urgency that is not relieved by drinking uva ursi, consult a practitioner promptly, as a kidney infection may be starting.

VALERIAN

USED SINCE ANCIENT TIMES as a nerve tonic and sedative, valerian has proved itself in modern-day clinical studies. Acting on the central nervous system, this herb restores mental balance and reduces anxiety. Valerian also relieves muscle spasms and tenseness.

HEALING PROPERTIES Phytochemicals called valepotriates originally appeared to be partially responsible for valerian's healing properties. Further studies have cast doubts on this, however, and suggest that numerous constituents, particularly in the essential oil, appear to work together. This herb successfully treats insomnia, nervousness, restlessness, and stress. It also may calm and soothe conditions such as hyperactivity, heart palpitations, tension headaches, nervous twitching, and even hysteria. And unlike sedatives, which often leave people feeling groggy, valerian does so pleasantly and usually without side effects.

This herb's relaxing actions also apply to muscle cramps, menstrual cramps, and high blood pressure, especially when associated with stress. Valerian is able to relax the smooth muscles that line artery walls, thus dilating the vessels and making it easier for the heart to pump blood through them.

Depression caused by long-term stress and nervous tension may be abated with use of this herb. Preliminary information indicates valerian may help calm hyperactive children.

TYPE OF PLANT Tall, stately valerian is a perennial plant. It has a characteristically erect, hairy stem that produces numerous pairs of leaves. Atop the thin stalks are small, whitish-pink to pinkish-purple flowers, which appear from early to midsummer. There are more than 200 varieties of valerian, some of them medicinal. *Valeriana officinalis* is one medicinal variety found growing in the United States.

HOW TO GROW Valerian seeds germinate poorly or not at all, so try to find a mature plant to divide. It overcrowds itself easily, so divide at least every three years. This herb grows easily in rich, moist soil with full sun to partial shade.

HARVESTING Gather roots, the medicinally useful part of this plant, in the fall. If you miss the timing, dig them up in the spring before new shoots appear.

PREPARATION AND DOSAGE Wash roots and let dry thoroughly. Use to make infusions or tinctures or powder to fill capsules. Valerian has such a disagreeable taste that you will need to mix it with pleasantly flavored herbs in order to drink it. You may wish to choose other herbs that also have a sedative effect, such as lemon balm and chamomile.

To alleviate daytime anxiety, high blood pressure, or muscle tension, take 1 or 2 capsules or ¾ teaspoon tincture several times per day. Doses may be increased slightly over time if needed.

Consume 1 cup of tea or 2 capsules or 1 teaspoon tincture one hour before bedtime for insomnia. It's safe to repeat the dose if it's not quite effective.

PRECAUTIONS Do not use valerian if you are pregnant.

Large doses (more than 4 cups of tea or several teaspoons of tincture) may cause headaches, dizziness, and heart palpitations. Occasionally, large doses will stimulate rather than sedate. In that case, discontinue use. Rarely, morning grogginess is reported after using valerian; if so, decrease the dosage.

WILD YAM IS an antispasmodic, anti-inflammatory, analgesic, diuretic, and expectorant—quite a lineup for a
lowly tuber. These healing properties are reflected in its
nicknames: rheumatism root and colicroot.

HEALING PROPERTIES Wild yam's
antispasmodic properties lessen
the pain of gallstones and kidney
stones, relieving spasms in the
muscular ducts leading out of
these organs. Other muscle
spasms, such as those that result
in stomach pain, intestinal
cramps, and menstrual cramps,
are also alleviated with the use
of this herb. Wild yam may help
prevent miscarriage if the uterus
starts to contract early.

Wild yam is especially good at
calming stomach cramps. It may
reduce flatulence, too. Its ability
to relax muscle spasms gives
relief to a baby with colic,
although it may be easier to get
a baby to drink fennel, mint, or
chamomile tea.

Wild yam contains compounds
called steroidal saponins that
reduce the inflammation of
rheumatoid arthritis as well as

natural analgesics that reduce
the pain of this uncomfortable
condition.

Wild yam has the false reputation of containing a natural form
of progesterone, a female hormone. This dates back to 1943
when a scientist made several
pounds of progesterone from
the wild Mexican yam (*Dioscorea
mexicana*) by extracting a
steroidal saponin called diosgenin from it. Diosgenin was
used as a base to make the
hormone. Up until 1970 this
was the only known way to
make the progesterone used in
contraceptive pills. It is not a
process that the body can
accomplish; it must be per-
formed in a laboratory.

TYPE OF PLANT Wild yam is a
perennial vine that is a good
climber. It has pleasing
heart-shaped leaves with small

hairs on their undersides. Wild yams produce slow-growing tubers. Medicinal properties come from the species *Dioscorea villosa* and perhaps others in the 600-member genus. Remember that the orange-colored potatoes often referred to as yams are only moist sweet potatoes, not true yams, which typically grow in the tropics.

HOW TO GROW In the wild this herb prefers moist, wooded areas. Try to duplicate these conditions if you cultivate wild yam. In the United States this plant is typically found from southern New England to Tennessee and westward to Texas.

HARVESTING It takes a minimum of four years for a plant to produce mature tubers. Dig them carefully at the end of the growing season.

PREPARATION AND DOSAGE

Dried root is decocted or powdered and put into capsules. Fresh or dried root is tinctured. Use 2–4 capsules per day or $\frac{1}{8}$–$\frac{1}{2}$ teaspoon tincture three to five times per day.

PRECAUTIONS No studies have been conducted showing wild yam is unsafe during pregnancy, and it has traditionally been used by pregnant women. Use caution and consult a midwife.

Reports indicate that wild yam has occasionally aggravated peptic ulcers. If you experience stomach or intestinal discomfort from taking wild yam, do not use it.

WITCH HAZEL

WITCH HAZEL IS A POPULAR astringent, toning and firming the skin, tightening pores, and removing excess oil. It can also stop discharge from oozing wounds and internal as well as external bleeding.

HEALING PROPERTIES Tannins, gallic acid, and essential oils give witch hazel its therapeutic properties. There are many conditions on this herb's healing list. For example, applied to an area with varicose veins or phlebitis (an inflamed vein), witch hazel is absorbed through the skin, soothing discomfort and temporarily tightening the vein. Applying a soft cloth soaked in strong witch hazel tea can also ease hemorrhoids. Properly made tincture, as described on page 189, can be taken internally to help these same conditions.

This herb's astringent qualities make it helpful for shrinking other tissues, too, such as a painful sore throat, although other herbs are more effective for sore throat. Just be sure not to use witch hazel preparations made with isopropyl alcohol.

Use a compress of witch hazel with arnica, a natural analgesic, to **externally** treat bruises and sprains. This herb is helpful for many skin conditions, such as rough, swollen hands; sunburn; insect bites; and rashes. Clinical trials have specifically shown that witch hazel, used topically, helps heal eczema and even may relieve vaginal infections when mixed with antimicrobial herbs.

TYPE OF PLANT Witch hazel is a small deciduous tree that may look more like a shrub. It has long, forked branches with twisting stems. Its bark is smooth, either gray or brown in color. The tree grows naturally in the Midwest and eastern portions of the United States, typically along streams or in moist, light woods.

HOW TO GROW In order to get seeds to germinate, they must be refrigerated for three months. It may be easier to start witch hazel from cuttings. This tree likes moist, rich soil that can be neutral or slightly acidic. It needs full sun to partial shade.

HARVESTING For best results, gather leaves, twigs, and bark early in the fall before the tree produces flowers.

PREPARATION AND DOSAGE
Dry or tincture your gathered bits of the witch hazel tree. Drink up to 3 cups of tea per day or take ½ teaspoon tincture two to six times per day. Do not use witch hazel continuously; limit its use to several weeks.

To make a lotion, start by making a tincture. Prune tree branches in the late fall or winter and remove bark. Cut into small chunks. Process in a blender or food processor along with small twigs and enough diluted vodka to cover the bark. Put into a glass jar. Store covered in a dark place for five or six weeks, shaking vigorously once a day. Strain. For every ounce of this witch hazel tincture, add ½ ounce aloe vera gel and ½ ounce vitamin E oil. Store in a glass jar.

PRECAUTIONS
Witch hazel contains tannins that can irritate the stomach if consumed frequently or in large quantities. Commercially prepared tinctures of this herb are sometimes prepared with rubbing (isopropyl) alcohol, which is poisonous. Read labels carefully. Be sure preparations made with rubbing alcohol are used for external purposes only.

WORMWOOD

WORMWOOD KILLS intestinal worms. Absinthin makes wormwood one of the most bitter plants known; thujone, a potent constituent, is a poison and convulsant.

HEALING PROPERTIES Originally, absinthin was used to make absinthe, an alcoholic drink that was addictive. It was banned when people realized that over-consumption of this liqueur caused irreversible nerve damage, mental impairment, and loss of reproductive function. However, it is this same bitter ingredient and others similar to it that, when used in small quantities, can stimulate digestion. Because it also stimulates peristalsis, the wavelike motion of the intestines that pushes food residue along, it may cause diarrhea. It appears to calm gallstone pain and relieve flatulence.

This herb kills intestinal worms and other internal parasites.

Pinworms, in particular, exit the intestine at night to lay eggs at the opening of the anus. To kill the eggs, dampen a cotton ball with wormwood oil and tuck it between the buttocks at night. This herb also repels fleas and moths.

Wormwood compresses or poultices may help bruises and sprains. Liniment with this herb has been used to relieve rheumatism and arthritis pain.

Its antiseptic and antibacterial properties make it useful for treating colds. A group of substances contained in wormwood called azulenes are anti-inflammatories and reduce fevers.

TYPE OF PLANT This hardy perennial offers an attractive profusion of fine, soft-looking, silver-green leaves. Its greenish-yellow flowers are inconspicuous and bloom in mid-summer. The plant is particularly handsome in autumn. It tolerates frost.

HOW TO GROW Summer is the time to plant this herb or to take cuttings. If you wish to divide the roots, do so in spring or fall. Wormwood needs an area that gets full sun. It's not picky about soil as long as it is alkaline. If your soil tends to be acidic, add a bit of lime.

HARVESTING Ideally, harvest the leaves before the plant has bloomed, although they may be useful afterwards. Use fresh or hang to dry. The flowering tops are less desirable because they are less effective; however, if you are using them, pick them just as the plant begins to bloom.

PREPARATION AND DOSAGE Use fresh wormwood to make tincture. Dry the leaves for tea infusions or to fill capsules. To make tea, use 1 teaspoon wormwood powder per cup of hot water. Steep 15 minutes. Drink before meals to improve digestion. If using capsules, take 1 before meals. However, this is a less desirable method as it bypasses the tongue, which is the strongest mediator of digestive stimulation through the vagus nerve. Some herbalists feel you should drink no more than $\frac{1}{2}$ cup of wormwood tea per day, taking only 1 teaspoon at a time. It is wise to start with small doses and see how your digestive system reacts.

Use tincture only for external purposes. It is rich in thujone, which is harmful to the nervous system.

PRECAUTIONS The U.S. Food and Drug Administration (FDA) classifies wormwood as dangerous. Do not use it if you are pregnant. Do not use internally for more than one or two days, and then only under the care of a qualified health care practitioner. Thujone is a convulsant, poison, and narcotic. Topical use is generally considered safe, although it may cause dermatitis in some people.

YARROW

SCIENCE HAS CONFIRMED that yarrow's traditional use for treating wounds to stop bleeding and prevent infection has merit. This herb contains several constituents that make blood coagulate, reduce pain and inflammation, and enhance healing.

HEALING PROPERTIES A heavy menstrual cycle or internal bleeding, such as that from ulcers, diminishes with use of this herb. For internal use, take tea or tinctures.

Along with promoting blood clotting, yarrow contains salicylic acid, the active ingredient in aspirin. Therefore this herb has analgesic properties, dulling the pain of the wounds it is treating. It has some antimicrobial function, too, helping to prevent wound infection.

This herb reduces external or internal inflammation with the same volatile oil found in chamomile—azulene. Its antispasmodic properties reduce spasms of the uterus along with those of the gallbladder. Being a bitter herb, it acts as a cholagogue, improving the flow of bile, enhancing digestion and helping prevent gallstones.

Yarrow helps break a fever by encouraging sweating, making it good therapy for colds and flu. It can dry up congestion from either respiratory infections or allergic reactions and is very helpful in intestinal flu as well.

Yarrow is used in aromatherapy to balance and give strength in times of major change, such as mid-life crisis or menopause or in the face of overwhelming emotions. It strengthens intuition.

TYPE OF PLANT Yarrow grows as a wild perennial throughout North America and in Europe and Asia, especially along roads, in empty lots, and in fallow fields. It's slender, reaching 2–3 feet in height. It has sparse, fine, feathery foliage and clusters of tiny white flowers, forming a head. It typically blooms June through September.

HOW TO GROW If starting from seed, do so in the spring. It's easy to divide; just find a mature plant in spring or fall. Yarrow is tolerant of most conditions; give it full sun and anything less than soggy soil.

HARVESTING Gather flowers while the plant is in bloom, preferably late spring and early summer; this is the portion of the plant most commonly used for medicinal purposes. Leaves may be gathered anytime. Dig roots in the fall.

PREPARATION AND DOSAGE Use yarrow flower heads fresh or dried for tea, tinctures, or to put into capsules. A gentle herb, you may drink up to 3 cups of tea or take ¼–1 teaspoon of tincture up to three times a day. Take 1 or 2 capsules two to five times per day.

Use infusions for skin washes. To clean wounds and stop bleeding, soak a cloth in a strong infusion of yarrow and apply it directly to the injury or sprinkle the powdered herb on it.

Mash fresh leaves and press over cuts to stop bleeding. Dried leaves or flowers can be used in the same manner.

Chewing on leaves or a piece of fresh yarrow root may relieve a toothache.

PRECAUTIONS This herb is generally considered safe and without side effects. Some experience contact dermatitis from touching the plant. A few people are allergic to yarrow, experiencing sneezing, nausea, or headache. If you are allergic to lactone or aspirin's salicylic acid, you may be allergic to this herb. Do not use it if you develop these symptoms.

Illnesses and Their Garden Healers

ARTERIOSCLEROSIS

COMMONLY CALLED hardening of the arteries, arteriosclerosis is a group of diseases characterized by thickened and hardened artery walls.

Atherosclerosis is a common type of arteriosclerosis in which fatty deposits partially clog or totally block blood flow in large, important vessels of the body such as the aorta and the blood vessels to the heart and head. As arteries throughout the body are affected, the heart has to pump harder than ever to circulate blood. This creates added stress on the heart, and the stage is set for heart disease. But many other diseases are associated with arteriosclerosis; the type of disease depends upon the artery that is clogged. If atherosclerosis affects the head, for instance, it can cause vision problems, dizziness, and stroke.

GARDEN HEALERS Your garden can help you reverse this health-robbing process. Tending your garden will ensure you get at least some physical activity, and just about every fruit, vegetable, and bean you grow contributes to good health. Rich in antioxidants, soluble fiber, flavonoids, potassium, and the B-vitamin folate, they also contain substances that improve blood flow, strengthen blood vessels, lower blood pressure, and relax the involuntary muscles inside the arteries that would otherwise cause arteries to go into spasm.

The more fruits and vegetables you eat, the fewer animal foods and processed foods you'll consume. Animal foods, typically high in saturated fat, should be eaten in small amounts, if at all. The body turns saturated fat into the type of cholesterol that thickens the blood and contributes to clogged arteries. Processed foods usually contain hydrogenated fat, which has caused even more severe damage than saturated fat in many studies. Complement your garden's bounty with whole grains.

The allium family is a star when it comes to fighting arteriosclerosis. Garlic and even onions have been clinically proved to reduce the "bad" LDL (low-density lipoprotein) cholesterol and increase the "good" HDL (high-density lipoprotein) cholesterol. Only raw or cooked garlic, not garlic oil, appears to have this effect. Press or chop the garlic so that its beneficial allicin is released. The key is breaking up the cells of the garlic.

Most produce from the garden is rich in soluble fiber and potassium. Soluble fiber is the type that helps lower blood cholesterol levels. Good sources include apples, carrots, cruciferous and nightshade vegetables (see food profiles), melons, sweet potatoes, and squash. Nearly all fresh fruits and vegetables contain potassium, which normalizes blood pressure and helps maintain a regular heartbeat.

Bioflavonoids are another important substance you can glean from the garden. These compounds strengthen the integrity of the blood vessels and help them retain their elasticity. This enables the heart to pump blood more easily. Flavonoids also have antioxidant abilities, preventing destroyer compounds called free radicals from damaging cells. In the case of heart disease, free radicals oxidize LDL cholesterol and fats in the bloodstream. Foods rich in these protective flavonoids include those that are particularly colorful, such as apricots, asparagus, beet greens, beets, all edible berries, citrus fruits, parsley, plums, dark-green salad greens, sweet potatoes, winter squash, and Swiss chard. Some of the garden's herbs and edible flowers, such as fennel, nettle, nasturtium, milk thistle, Oregon grape, rosemary, and skullcap, are rich in flavonoids, too.

Free radicals manifest from many sources, such as polluted air, ultraviolet light, rancid foods, and oil heated to high temperatures. Luckily, the body knows how to use antioxidants to get rid of these rascals. Vitamins A, C, and E and the carotenes and flavonoids all help protect cells from damage.

Horsetail's abundant supply of minerals may also strengthen vessel walls. Additionally, it may guard against fatty deposits in the arteries. Many fresh fruits and vegetables are also rich in folate, another nutrient recognized for helping to prevent heart disease. Along with vitamins B_6 and B_{12}, folate helps reduce levels of homocysteine, a compound associated with a higher risk of heart attack. Good sources of folate include dark leafy greens, citrus fruits, watercress, and hot peppers. The other B vitamins, B_6 and B_{12}, are found primarily in protein foods; sunflower seeds are rich in B_6.

Some herbs help increase blood flow, reduce blood "stickiness," and improve circulation. Researchers have found that Ginkgo biloba is one such herb that reduces the risk of heart

attacks, although it is not grown in most gardens because it is a slow-growing tree. However, you can plant it and collect your own leaves in a few years. Angelica, cayenne, juniper, nettle, and rosemary also jump-start circulation. All clovers contain coumarin, a compound that protects blood vessels.

Skullcap has been studied in Russia, where it was found to stabilize heart disease that is linked to stress factors. American researchers recently discovered that psychological stress activates a certain part of the brain in some people that can then trigger heart attacks. Perhaps skullcap's calming abilities interfere with this reaction. In Japan, scientists have verified that this herb increases "good" HDL cholesterol levels.

Valerian is also known for its ability to reduce elevated blood pressure when caused by stress, and it relaxes blood vessel walls, preventing spasm and ultimately enhancing blood flow. Lemon balm is another calming herb that has similar actions.

ARTHRITIS

THIS PAINFUL and debilitating joint disease is usually either classified as osteoarthritis (OA) or rheumatoid arthritis (RA).

OA is a condition in which the cartilage of the joints slowly deteriorates and hardens. Bone spurs often form in the area of the joint, resulting in deformity and limited mobility. Inflammation is not present or is minimal. OA most commonly affects those age 65 and older.

Unlike OA, RA is characterized by inflammation of the membranes surrounding joints; they become tender and swollen. It is an autoimmune disorder, which means that the body's immune system is attacking its own tissues. RA most often strikes people between the ages of 20 and 40, crippling more women than men. RA often attacks joints in a symmetrical fashion, e.g., both hands or both knees. Joints can become deformed.

GARDEN HEALERS Horsetail's cornucopia of minerals, including silicon, may nourish joint cartilage. Ample amounts of tissue-building minerals in your daily diet will keep bones healthy and may help prevent bone spurs, a common complication of arthritis. Researchers have reported that people with RA who follow a predominantly lacto-ovo vegetarian diet (includes eggs and dairy products but no meats) for one year notice significant improvements.

In some people, arthritic conditions seem to be related to food allergies or sensitivities to common foods including wheat and dairy. Others believe that foods from the nightshade family, such as tomatoes, potatoes, and peppers, aggravate their condition, although others don't notice any connection. If you think certain foods play a role in your arthritis symptoms, it is important to put them to the test. Eliminate suspect foods for one week and nightshades for several months. Add eliminated foods back into your diet, one at a time, every four days. Note any reactions. During such trial and error times, be careful to keep eating a nutritionally balanced diet to support your body's healing efforts. It may be necessary to do a more exten-

sive elimination or challenge to identify multiple allergenic foods. Consult a nutritionally oriented physician for guidance on how to attempt this safely and effectively.

Some garden herbs act as analgesics, relieving pain. But do not try to eliminate all pain entirely, as it's a reminder to rest joints that are experiencing stress. Other herbs help to reduce inflammation, protect and support joint cartilage, and remove toxins that may accumulate in joints.

Pain-relieving herbs include cayenne pepper. Although it's in the nightshade family, arthritis sufferers are typically not bothered by it. A cream made from peppers is most effective, and multiple clinical studies show it works for people with osteoarthritis and rheumatoid arthritis. Arnica, which is used externally only, is a moderately strong pain reliever. Mint, wild yam, and yarrow are mild analgesics. Make a tea out of one or more of the latter three. Use

---

ARTHRITIS RECIPES

HORSERADISH POULTICE

Use fresh horseradish root. Process with enough hot water in a blender to make a thick paste. Soak a piece of thin cotton fabric in hot water, then spread the horseradish root mixture onto the cloth. Cover with a second layer of dry cotton fabric. Place the moist side of the poultice over a sore joint. Leave on for 15–30 minutes. Use a hot water bottle on top of the poultice to keep it hot. If it becomes uncomfortable, remove the poultice. It is normal for the skin to redden, as the heat increases circulation in the affected area.

JUNIPER COMPRESS

Make a strong infusion with juniper berries or their tincture. Soak a cloth in the warm liquid. Apply to aching joints.

arnica in a massage oil or ointment to rub into sore spots. Do the same with cayenne, juniper, rosemary, chamomile, or thyme.

There is a bountiful supply of anti-inflammatories in the garden that can help RA. Foods such as apples, parsley, and hot peppers help decrease inflammation. There are many herbs that also reduce inflammation of tissues and joints. Chamomile, elderberry, feverfew, goldenseal, licorice, marshmallow, nettle, skullcap, wild yam, wormwood, and yarrow all have compounds that fight inflammation. Pick a few of these herbs that are suited to your climate and will fit into your herb garden. Make an infusion of several and sip as tea. Combine with other pleasant-tasting herbs if you prefer. Refer to the individual herb profiles for guidance on which plant parts to use and how to prepare them.

Some physicians speculate that toxins in the system may irritate joints and prevent cartilage from forming normally. In this case,

diuretics may help by flushing out toxins. Herbal diuretics include parsley, hydrangea, burdock, dandelion, horsetail, and goldenrod. Brew a tea of one or several of these. When using diuretic herbs, be sure to eat plenty of fruits and vegetables that are rich in potassium—just in case your body gets rid of too much potassium as it eliminates excess water. The best source is dandelion leaves. Running low on potassium can precipitate a heart attack and even death. Your heart needs this mineral to keep beating regularly and to normalize blood pressure.

Do not use juniper if you have kidney disease. Wormwood should be used only in small amounts for short periods of time.

BENIGN PROSTATIC HYPERPLASIA (BPH)

THIS CONDITION IS commonly referred to as an enlarged prostate gland. Typically occurring in half

of men over the age of 50 in the United States, an enlarged prostate gland sometimes makes urination difficult.

BPH may be accompanied by frequent urges to urinate and sometimes by partial incontinence. It is not predictive of prostate cancer, but its presence is still disturbing, and it should be monitored by a health care professional who can determine whether it is a benign condition or cancer.

GARDEN HEALERS The healing garden offers several remedies for BPH. Tea, tincture, or capsules of hydrangea root or horsetail are often used to reduce the inflammation of the prostate gland. Nettle root tincture or capsules are also helpful. In fact, scientific studies have proved its ability to diminish this enlarged gland. Amounts used in successful studies range from 6–12 mL of tincture per day in divided doses, or 120 mg capsules twice a day.

Saw palmetto, a very beneficial and well-studied herb, provides great therapy for the enlarged prostate. In fact, one study showed significant improvement in 45 days with only mild or no side effects. However, saw palmetto is a wild palm tree that grows in swamps of the southeastern United States—so it's not likely to be in your garden or landscape. For best results, you may wish to use a combination of all the herbs mentioned. Since excessive consumption of animal products increases the risk of BPH, eating more vegetables and fruits of all kinds is likely to be beneficial.

A hormone imbalance is usually the cause of an enlarged prostate. Although the body normally turns ordinary testosterone into a very potent form called dihydrotestosterone (DHT), it can cause an enlargement when there is too much DHT. Wrapping around the urethra, the tube that allows urine to exit the bladder, a swollen prostate gland acts like a clamp, sometimes resulting in problems with urination. Men may need to get up several times a night to urinate or have the sensation of a full bladder even after urinating. Frequent urges result only in dribbling urination that has little force. If the urethra is too impaired, urine may back up throughout the urinary system. This significantly increases the risk of a urinary tract infection and/or kidney damage.

The mineral zinc may halt the processing of testosterone into DHT and thus may prevent or even reverse the condition. Pumpkin seeds from your garden are an excellent source of zinc, especially if you fertilize with kelp, and may contain other helpful substances as well. Eating 2 ounces of pumpkin seeds per day significantly boosts your zinc intake. Some people prefer to take zinc supplements for BPH. If you decide to supplement with zinc, use no more than 50 mg per day for three months and include a copper supplement of 2 mg per day. These two minerals compete for

absorption—zinc will win out and cause a copper deficiency if you're not careful. Look for a zinc supplement that includes copper.

✂ An enlarged prostate gland should be diagnosed only by a health care practitioner to rule out prostate cancer. Get a thorough lab workup to ensure you are dealing only with an enlarged prostate. If you have Wilson disease, you should not use copper supplements.

BITES AND STINGS

INSECT BITES and stings are particularly common during the summer—luckily, the same time your healing garden is at its peak. An herb garden can take away the "ouch" after a bite or sting.

GARDEN HEALERS A poultice of fresh plantain leaves is the easiest and safest remedy for mosquito bites and wasp stings. Plantain is an extremely common weed in yards and gardens but serves as an excellent medicine. Simply chew up a leaf (from a plant not sprayed with chemicals) and apply it to the sting.

Lavender oil is indispensable for this purpose. Keep it on hand to ease the discomfort of insect bites; rub a little onto the affected area. To make lavender oil, cover finely chopped lavender flowers with ¼ inch vegetable oil; gently heat lavender and oil together until the mixture is warm and fragrant. Strain and store in a cool dark place. This mixture retains its healing properties for about six months.

Mosquito bites and wasp stings can also be treated with a lotion made of witch hazel, or use a strong infusion of plantain or witch hazel as a soothing wash. A swab of mint tea will put a stop to itching. Both chamomile and goldenrod poultices are very effective in preventing redness and swelling.

For bee stings, after the stinger is removed, run cold water over the stung area and then apply a paste made of baking soda or a plantain poultice. Use lavender oil later to calm the stinging. A marshmallow root or seed poultice soothes the inflammation and irritation that accompanies a sting.

A few herbs may help repel insects, possibly preventing bites and stings from occurring in the first place. Applied externally, wormwood, lavender, and citronella will deter some pesky bugs. Wormwood is especially good for fleas, whereas lavender and citronella work well against mosquitoes. Infuse their essences into oils or creams, and apply to skin.

⅄ If you have severe or allergic reactions to bee or wasp stings, seek medical attention immediately.

BLOOD PRESSURE

CLOGGING OF the blood vessels combined with excessive constriction are the major problems behind elevated blood pressure. This blockage

puts stress on the heart, causing it to beat harder to push the blood. This can eventually lead to heart attack, stroke, and even kidney failure.

Blood pressure readings above 140/90 mm Hg are considered high, and those over 130/80 mm Hg are suboptimal. Low blood pressure carries few known long-term health risks but can produce symptoms such as fainting and dizziness upon standing.

GARDEN HEALERS To reduce high blood pressure, it's important to eat fewer foods rich in sodium if you are sensitive to this mineral. Processed foods account for 80 percent of the sodium in most diets. It is helpful to increase the amount of potassium, calcium, and magnesium in your diet. Most vegetables and fruits in the garden are rich in potassium. Broccoli and dark leafy greens are full of magnesium and calcium, except for spinach and Swiss chard, whose calcium is

unavailable for absorption. Researchers have found that celery contains a substance that lowers blood pressure; the Chinese have used celery for this purpose for centuries.

Garlic helps lower blood pressure by keeping the arteries clear of cholesterol and potential plaque buildup. It also decreases blood clotting and widens the arteries. Hawthorn berries and ginkgo biloba are reputed to dilate arteries, too, making the heart's job of pushing blood through them a little easier.

Passion flower, valerian, limeflower (*Tilia cordata*), and lemon balm have sedative properties, so if your blood pressure condition is thought to be connected to stress and anxiety, tranquilizing herbs such as these can lend a hand without side effects. Valerian also relaxes the smooth muscles that line the artery walls, preventing them from constricting.

Low blood pressure can be treated with herbs that stimulate

circulation. Cayenne pepper, horseradish, and angelica may be helpful. Licorice tea may also increase blood pressure.

BURNS, MINOR

PLANTS FROM the healing garden can help treat burns and scalds. First, though, you need to cool off the skin. Immediately put the injured area under cold running water to dissipate the heat and arrest tissue damage.

Once the site is cooled, several herbs can help diminish pain and heal the injury. If the burn is large, blisters severely, or is painless, seek emergency help.

GARDEN HEALERS The aloe plant is a renowned burn healer. Keep a plant indoors on a shady windowsill for prompt use on the minor burns and scalds that inevitably occur in the kitchen. Snip off a leaf tip and squeeze its juice onto the burn. For larger burns, neatly trim an outer leaf off the plant. Slice through one side of the leaf lengthwise and

scoop out the healing gel. Apply directly to afflicted skin. If you wish, put the gel in a small jar and mix a little vitamin E oil in with it. Vitamin E makes a good natural burn healer.

Lavender oil is a useful treatment for burns or scalds. Gently apply it to the affected area. St. John's wort oil will also help skin heal and decrease associated inflammation.

Witch hazel, elder flowers, and comfrey are also herbal burn remedies. Make a strong infusion of any of these. Wet clean gauze with witch hazel decoction and bind it to the scalded or burned area. Apply elder flower or comfrey leaves and flowers directly to the burn.

Taken internally, vitamin C promotes wound healing by helping the body produce strong collagen, the base material for new skin. Eat plenty of raw garden produce such as broccoli, bell peppers, leafy greens, potatoes, melons, berries, and citrus fruits to help burns heal from the inside out.

CANCER

CANCER CAN STRIKE anyone, anywhere, at any-time in life. The good news is that many cancers are diet-or lifestyle-related. This means you have the power to take preventative steps that will lower your risk.

GARDEN HEALERS Whole, unprocessed foods from your garden are naturals when it comes to preventing cancer. Rich in the vitamins and minerals that keep your immune system primed—which is your first line of defense against cancer—these foods also contain substances that can nip cancer before it gets started. Most garden produce is full of the antioxidant vitamins A and C, carotenoids, and flavonoids. Depending on your soil, they may also be rich in the antioxidant mineral selenium. Antioxidants stop free radicals, preventing them from damaging DNA and mutating cells, which are often the start of cancer.

High fiber foods from the garden, such as oats, other whole grains, and many vegetables, help prevent colon and rectal cancers.

Cruciferous vegetables contain substances called indoles and sulphoraphane, both of which are well-known cancer fighters. Broccoli sprouts appear to be the best source of these helpful compounds. One way these phytochemicals work is to help rid the body of excess estrogen, which is related to breast and other hormone-related cancers. Preliminary animal studies indicate that indoles may not only help prevent this disease but also may keep it from spreading. People who eat several servings a week of cruciferous vegetables have a much lower risk of many cancers than those who don't.

The dark green and yellow-orange fruits and vegetables contain the anticancer carotenoid team. Many of these are more powerful antioxidants than beta-carotene. Lycopene, found predominantly in red-colored foods such as tomatoes, pink grapefruit, and watermelon, is particularly good at preventing prostate cancer. Other potent carotenoids include zeaxanthin, alpha-carotene, cryptoxanthin, and lutein.

Brightly colored purple and red vegetables and fruits are rich in flavonoids, which are powerful antioxidants. Many flavonoids also boost immune function. Berries, plums, and red cabbage are good examples, although onions and parsley are also rich in these compounds. Proanthocyanidins and quercetin are some of the more widely known flavonoids.

One herb that appears to help the immune system stay primed to seek out and destroy mutated cells is echinacea.

Several herbs are being studied for their potential use in the war on cancer. The National Cancer Institute is looking into St. John's wort for this purpose. Red clover contains a substance

called biochanin A, which may help prevent cancer. Scientists have isolated several compounds in red clover that have anti-tumor properties. Some of aloe vera's phytochemicals also show promise in treating this dreaded disease. In years to come, science will undoubtedly discover and confirm more anticancer properties of nature's plants.

CANKER AND COLD SORES

THESE ARE actually two different conditions. Canker sores are white ulcers with a reddened rim around them. Cold sores, on the other hand, are small, clear blisters that typically occur on the edge of the lips. They break open and usually form a yellowish crust.

Canker sores can be caused by a run-in with your toothbrush, braces that irritate a certain place, ill-fitting dentures, food allergies, mineral deficiencies, rough fillings, and in some cases, nutritional deficiencies.

Cold sores are caused by a specific strain of the herpes virus, which can lie dormant for long periods of time, then flare up after stress, illness, or sometimes sun exposure.

GARDEN HEALERS Herbs that are effective in healing canker sores include Oregon grape root, echinacea, and chamomile. Lemon balm, along with these, is helpful for herpes.

Licorice is best applied topically or taken internally for short periods while cold sores are present. Licorice root tea and a commercial preparation known as deglycyrrhizinated licorice (DGL for short) have been shown to help canker sores as well, with no chance of elevating blood pressure. Make infusions of any of the recommended herbs and use as a mouthwash, gently swishing them in the mouth for a couple of minutes to help shorten the healing time.

Cold sores need to be treated by herbs that have antiviral properties. Lemon balm and St. John's wort are particularly helpful in

killing the herpes virus. Use them as a tincture to dab onto areas as soon as you first notice the tingling that often precedes a cold sore. Use it several times daily if the sore manifests. Commercially available, highly concentrated creams may be applied as well.

Oregon grape is an antiviral, too. Licorice also keeps viruses from replicating, so it can be used for cold sores as well as canker sores. Infusions of any of these herbs may help diminish activity of this unwanted "bug."

COLD SORE RECIPE

1 tablespoon fresh lemon balm (or freeze-dried)

1 cup boiling water

Pour boiling water over lemon balm. Let steep 15 minutes. Drink as a tea, hot or cold. It is safe to consume as much lemon balm tea as you want. Several cups a day may help keep the herpes virus in check. Do not use dried lemon balm unless you just picked and dried it yourself and it still has a strong lemony smell, as its active ingredients are lost in the slow-drying process; freeze-drying retains them.

CANKER SORE RECIPE

¼ teaspoon powdered
licorice root

¾ cup lukewarm water

Stir the licorice root into the water. Hold in the mouth and swish for two to three minutes, then spit out. Repeat each morning and evening until sores have healed.

Echinacea and other immune boosters can help the body fend off the herpes virus. Echinacea also contains a substance that protects collagen, the basis of skin and mucous membranes, from breakdown by bacterial and viral enzymes. Taken internally it may help these types of sores heal more quickly. Swish about 1 teaspoon of strong echinacea root decoction or ½ teaspoon tincture in the mouth for several minutes, then swallow. Repeat three times per day or more.

Chamomile contains a substance called bisabolol that helps heal sores of the mucous membranes and is antimicrobial as well. It also contains chamazulene, an anti-inflammatory substance.

CATARACTS

A CATARACT is a clouding or opacity of the lens of the eye, making it difficult to see through.

Often age-related, cataracts occur in most people who live long enough. That's because the eye undergoes a lifetime of bombardment by sunlight's ultraviolet rays, which create free radicals in the eye. These free radicals cause cell damage, leading to cataracts. Smokers and persons who have diabetes have an increased risk of developing cataracts, as do those who are exposed to excessive amounts of sunlight.

Antioxidants are a natural defense against this condition. Smokers use antioxidants at a high rate because cigarette smoke creates an enormous number of free radicals. Many studies show that people who have lower levels of antioxidants in their bloodstream and in the lens of the eye have a higher incidence of cataracts.

People with diabetes, however, develop cataracts differently. They tend to have higher than normal levels of sugar in the bloodstream and eye. This puts extra pressure on the lens, making it inflexible and eventually damaging cells to the point of cataract formation.

GARDEN HEALERS To prevent development of cataracts because of free radical damage, eat garden produce that is rich in antioxidants. Bell and hot peppers, melons, cabbages, potatoes, berries, and citrus fruits are all rich in vitamin C; most items from the garden contain good amounts. Vitamin E is less common in plants. Sweet potatoes however, are unusual in that they contain quite a bit of vitamin E. Beta-carotene and other carotenoids also battle free radicals. Beta-carotene is prevalent in sweet potatoes, too, as well as in winter squash, carrots, apricots, melons with orange-colored flesh, and dark, leafy greens. A carotenoid called lutein is a powerful antioxidant, and spinach is chock-full of it.

Flavonoids in berries and other purple- and red-colored fruits also put a stop to free radical damage. Quercetin, a flavonoid, helps people with diabetes by preventing sugars from accumulating in the eye. Cabbage family vegetables, especially broccoli, overflow with antioxidants such as lutein and quercetin.

The berries of the bilberry plant are rich in anthocyanidins, another potent flavonoid free-radical fighter. It protects not only the lens but also the back of the eye, the retina. To get hefty doses of this substance, the extract, capsules, or tablets are often used, sometimes as much as 240–480 mg per day. There are no known problems or side effects associated with taking bilberry in these amounts.

Bilberry contains antioxidant flavonoids, which help keep cataracts at bay, but it also carries substances in its leaves that may help lower and stabilize blood sugar in people with diabetes. Similarly, much of the garden produce that contains fiber, especially soluble fiber, will also help a person with diabetes control blood sugar levels. Good sources include apricots, apples, beets, berries, citrus fruits, parsnips, squash, and oats, to name just a few. Adequately controlling blood sugar may reduce complications of diabetes such as cataracts.

COLDS AND COUGH

UNFORTUNATELY, a cold must run its course through sneezing fits, sore throat, and congestion. But there are plants in your healing garden that can reduce the congestion and length and severity of your next cold or prevent one from taking hold.

GARDEN HEALERS When you first begin to feel a cold coming on, support and stimulate your body's immune system. Use tinctures or capsules of echinacea and goldenseal to help produce extra white blood cells that can destroy the intruding virus. You may be able to avoid the cold entirely if your defenses

are mounted early enough. But if not, your cold will probably be milder and shorter. Take up to 600–900 mg echinacea in capsule form or 4 mL (¾ teaspoon) extract three to six times per day. Garden products such as garlic, onions, and cayenne are also known as anti-virals; eat plenty of these fresh to keep your defenses up. Other herbs from your garden that will energize immunity include aloe, chamomile, licorice, Oregon grape, marshmallow, and skullcap.

Echinacea can be taken at a dose of ½ teaspoon three times daily to prevent colds.

Eat plenty of fruits and vegetables that are loaded with vitamin C, such as citrus fruits, melons, berries, watercress, parsley, and bell peppers. Vitamin C acts as a mild natural antihistamine while also supporting the function of white blood cells. Antihistamines reduce mucus secretion and inflammation in airways and sinuses, making it easier for you to breathe.

To help break up the congestion in lungs and sinuses, use plants with expectorant properties. Try hot peppers, horseradish, lavender, mullein, mint, red clover, rosemary, and elder flowers. Many of these herbs do double duty. For instance, the demulcent properties in mullein, as well as marshmallow, help soothe an aching throat and calm a cough. The capsaicin in cayenne pepper diminishes pain messages from nerve endings, offering relief from sore throat pain; use it in a gargle. Gargle teas or tinctures of these plants for maximum relief.

Some of your garden's aromatherapy plants can be infused into massage oil, then rubbed into your chest. Lavender, peppermint, and yarrow can all alleviate congestion. Lavender may also stimulate immune function and induce much-needed sleep. Yarrow and elder flowers can promote sweating and help break a fever.

Gargling with mucilaginous herbs relieves an irritated throat

COMMON COLD RECIPE

To reduce congestion and help clear sinuses, try a steam treatment.

1. Put lavender, eucalyptus, or mint in a medium-sized bowl; use 8 drops if you have essential oil.

2. Pour 2 cups of steaming hot water over the herbs or oil.

3. Cover your head with a towel, lean over the bowl, and slowly breath in the steam.

4. Blow your nose gently as mucus is loosened.

5. Continue to breathe steam for about five minutes.

and constant cough. Use a strong, warm infusion as a gargle. Try marshmallow, licorice, red raspberry, or calendula to soothe the irritation and make swallowing a little easier.

✂ If you are pregnant, do not use the common cold recipe above except with chamomile flowers. Use only 4 drops essential oil for children. Close your eyes to avoid irritation. Use caution as steam can burn.

See the individual herb profiles for dosage amounts and precautions.

CONSTIPATION

CONSTIPATION is a condition characterized by infrequent bowel movements (a change in your usual pattern); dry, hard stools that are difficult to pass; an inability to move the bowels when desired; and abdominal discomfort.

It's estimated that one-third of all Americans contend with constipation on a somewhat regular basis. Lack of fiber, water, and exercise can precipitate constipation. Many medications also contribute to this condition. Regardless of how often constipation plagues you, the healing garden can help.

GARDEN HEALERS First of all, be sure to eat plenty of high fiber foods—all the vegetables and fruits from your garden plus whole grains. Avoid refined flour products, processed foods, and all animal products, as they tend to be low in fiber. Fibrous root vegetables such as carrots and parsnips are bursting with this undigestible substance, espe-cially the insoluble kind that sweeps the colon clean. Drinking 6–8 glasses of water each day and walking for 30 minutes may be all your sluggish colon needs to get back on track.

If that doesn't do the trick, laxatives might. There are two main categories of laxatives: Those that add bulk and those that stimulate contractions in the bowels.

The bulking laxatives are rich in fiber and mucilage that expands when combined with water. The increased volume in the colon creates natural contractions that push food residue through. Be sure to consume large quantities of water, at least 2 cups, with these high fiber laxatives. These are the preferred types of laxative, as they are not habit forming and do not generally make the colon dependent. Typical bulk-forming laxatives include psyllium seeds and husks, flaxseed, and fenugreek—not common in a garden but widely available.

However, you can grow the other type of laxatives. Take only small amounts and only use them occasionally. Regular use can make you dependent on them and cause dehydration and potassium depletion. Stimulant laxatives contain substances called anthraquinones that irritate the colon muscles, making them contract. Examples of this type of laxative include senna, cascara bark, and aloe. Some of these are very potent and cause painful cramping. Aloe should be used with caution, as it contains an extremely strong laxative in the yellow portion right beneath the peel of the leaf. It can cause diarrhea. Only commercially prepared aloe has this potent compound removed; its mucilaginous gel may serve as a lubricant. Senna is another popular laxative that is commonly used too frequently. In large amounts, senna can cause cramping. Cascara bark is a milder but still potent stimulating herb. All these potent irritant laxatives should not be used regularly as their strong effects easily make the colon less responsive to milder stimulation, thus compounding the problem.

Dandelion root is perhaps the mildest laxative in this category. Burdock, eaten as a vegetable, tea, or tincture, is also a gentle laxative. The Chinese have long prescribed it for constipation. Marshmallow has been used for centuries to treat constipation. Its soothing demulcent quality provides lubrication in the colon and calms inflammation.

Dried plums, or prunes, are well-known for their ability to combat constipation. Plant an Italian prune plum tree, pick the ripe fruit, and dry them or eat them fresh. Rich in fiber and a natural sugar called sorbitol, prunes have the ability to promote bowel movements virtually every time. Researchers developed a jam using prunes and dates for hospitalized patients. It was so successful that many other institutions have adopted the recipe, which is

LAXATIVE JAM RECIPE

1 cup pitted prunes

1 cup pitted dates

1 cup boiling water

Bring water to a boil in a medium-sized saucepan. Cut or chop dates and prunes into small pieces. Add to boiling water, and cook until mixture is thick. Use 1 tablespoon per day. Yield: Approximately 20 tablespoons.

shown above. Black cherry juice is also helpful in the same way.

Which type of laxative should you use? Generally there are two types of constipation. Flaccid constipation is characterized by weak muscular activity in the colon. This condition is the one that usually responds to bulking agents and increased physical activity. Abdominal massage, a high fiber diet, and certain herbs can help this type of constipation. Make an infusion or decoction (remember, an infusion is used for upper parts of a plant, whereas a decoction is used for the root) of one part each of licorice root, raspberry leaves,

and Oregon grape root. Add two parts dandelion root.

Tense, over-contracted muscles in the colon characterize the second type of constipation. This type responds to herbs that help relax the muscles of the bowel so that residue can be pushed on through. Again, make an infusion or decoction of the following herbs: one part each of chamomile, valerian, and peppermint mixed with two parts each of licorice, wild yam, and dandelion root.

For all types of constipation, psyllium seeds are recommended. They are a gentle yet effective bulk laxative.

ᛣ Some people experience allergic reactions (skin and respiratory) when exposed to psyllium seed. Do not use dandelion root if you have large gallstones. Avoid using senna or any of the other stimulating laxatives for more than ten consecutive days or they may cause dependency. Chronic use of these herbs can also result in diarrhea, dehydration, depressed potassium levels, and irregular heartbeat. Do not use stimulating laxatives if you are pregnant or have Crohn disease, ulcerative colitis, or inflammatory bowel disease.

CUTS, SCRATCHES, ABRASIONS

IT'S MOST IMPORTANT to clean wounds promptly with soap and water to prevent infections. The healing process can then be accelerated and the potential for infection can be reduced by using many herbs.

GARDEN HEALERS Herbs for treating cuts, scratches, and abrasions include those that help fight infectious microbes, decrease inflammation, soothe the pain, and help the wound to heal.

Garlic juice applied to infected wounds hastens healing. The allicin in garlic has been shown to be as effective as a one percent penicillin solution. However, it may cause damage to the skin, so be cautious. Lavender, scented geranium, and rosemary are good antiseptics, too. Use diluted tinctures or diluted essential oils.

Calendula's strong infusion also makes an effective compress. Chamomile flower infusion will reduce swelling and prevent infection. A poultice of marshmallow will help shallow cuts heal. Since it can promote the growth of microbes, only leave it on for up to 30 minutes.

Teas made of echinacea, wormwood, Oregon grape, and goldenseal, when applied topically to the cut or abrasion, help prevent infection. Juniper leaves and berries have been used externally for generations to treat infections and wounds while yarrow has been traditionally used for cleaning wounds and helping blood clot faster in cuts. Witch hazel and cayenne pepper also stop bleeding and promote healing. A compress of St. John's wort will work on deeper cuts.

If cuts are very deep or gaping or if there is any risk of tetanus (when wounds are caused by any object contaminated with soil), get medical attention. Do not treat large open wounds with herbs.

DEPRESSION

DEPRESSION is characterized by feelings of sadness, inadequacy, and indifference that last for long periods of time.

Brought on by a variety of factors ranging from chemical imbalances in the brain to prolonged stress or a traumatic event, untreated depression can have life-threatening consequences.

GARDEN HEALERS St. John's wort is perhaps the most well-known herb for treating depression. It has been clinically studied extensively. Various studies show St. John's wort significantly improves depression and relieves anxiety after taking it four to six weeks. Capsules containing 300 mg (standardized to 0.3 percent hypericin) taken three times per day are beneficial. Side effects from St. John's wort are very rare. St. John's wort tea or tincture can also be used if you grow it in your garden and make the preparations out of fresh plants.

Good nourishment in general is important for preventing and treating depression. The brain needs nutrients to make necessary chemicals called neurotransmitters. Adequate intake of B vitamins is essential, particularly B_6 and folate. Sunflower seeds are rich in B_6 while vegetables such as asparagus, parsnips, citrus fruits, beets, spinach, and other dark leafy greens are packed with folate.

Pumpkin seeds provide a high level of the amino acid tryptophan, which in the brain promotes the synthesis of a neurotransmitter called serotonin. Normal levels of serotonin provide a calm sense of well-being.

Aromatherapy can be useful for lifting the spirits. Use an aromatherapy lamp to infuse a room with scent or tuck a scented cloth into your pillowcase at night. Scented geranium, lavender, angelica, chamomile, juniper, mint, and rosemary are all good choices. Infusing their essences into massage oil is another enjoyable way to beat depression.

Ginkgo biloba helps the brain make certain neurotransmitters, which may alleviate depression. One study has shown a standardized extract was helpful for elderly, depressed persons who also had dementia. Even the lowly oat, fresh in its milky stage and made into a tincture, has a reputation as a nerve tonic and can diminish cravings associated with addictions.

In rare cases, taking doses of St. John's wort that are higher than those recommended for prolonged periods may cause sensitivity to sunlight, especially in fair-skinned people; a rash may result from exposure to sun. Avoid cheese, red wine, yeast, and pickled herring if taking St. John's wort, and do not use along with prescription antidepressants without consulting an expert botanical prescriber. Do not take St. John's wort if you're pregnant, since this is a time for extra caution, even though this herb is probably safe.

DIABETES

THIS CONDITION IS **characterized by the body's inability to move digested carbohydrates and sugars into cells.**

Insulin, a protein hormone, is necessary to shuttle the nutrients into the cells. People with diabetes either no longer make insulin, don't make enough of it, or their cells stop responding to it no matter how much of it is present.

Diabetes that strikes people younger than age 20 is usually Type I, or juvenile-onset diabetes. Researchers think this is an autoimmune disorder in which the body has destroyed its own insulin-making cells. These people must take insulin on a daily basis and watch their diet carefully.

Those diagnosed with diabetes after 20 years of age usually have Type II, or adult-onset diabetes. These people are often, but not always, overweight. Their insulin-making cells still work, but they either don't make enough of this hormone or the body's other cells have become desensitized to it. Treatment often includes weight reduction and oral medications to stimulate insulin production.

GARDEN HEALERS Regardless of whether a person has Type I or II diabetes, it's important to keep an eye on blood sugar levels. Having too much sugar in the bloodstream eventually damages organs throughout the body. Not having enough blood sugar can result in mental confusion and even coma and death if severe enough.

Eating a diet rich in fiber helps the body absorb sugars slowly, which in turn keeps blood sugar levels on a more even keel. Most of the vegetables and fruits in your garden are rich in fiber. The soluble type of fiber, the one that does the best job of stabilizing blood sugar levels, is abundant in apples, apricots, beets, berries, carrots, citrus fruits, parsnips, and winter squash, to name a few. Oats are extremely rich in soluble fiber; their bran makes a good addition to cereals and baked goods. Soluble fiber is also helpful in lowering elevated LDL cholesterol levels, a serious problem in many people with diabetes.

Consume garlic and onions in large quantities. These flavorful foods help to lower "bad" LDL cholesterol and raise "good" HDL cholesterol and prevent heart disease. People with diabetes tend to have a greater risk of heart disease because the lack of insulin prompts fat to float throughout the bloodstream longer and in higher levels than normal. Eat a diet abundant in vegetables and moderate in sweet fruits to get a rich array of antioxidants such as vitamin C, the carotenes, and flavonoids. Antioxidants help prevent fats from oxidizing and causing damage to artery walls, which can lead to plaque buildup and heart disease.

Basil leaves have been shown to lower blood sugar levels. Cactus juice from pods, sometimes found in produce markets or grown in arid climates, is also helpful.

The leaves of the bilberry plant are known to lower blood sugar levels, but don't try to self-medicate your diabetes—contact a nutritionally trained health care provider before changing your regimen. The berries of this wild perennial help people with diabetes avoid some of the typical complications that are usually related to diminished blood circulation. They have compounds in them that improve circulation and help keep blood cells from clumping together. Their flavonoids keep tiny blood capillaries strong so blood can continue to circulate to all parts of the body.

The leaves of the fig tree are a very useful blood–sugar-lowering treatment. Fig trees can be grown in warmer climates. Use caution if you are taking insulin or an oral hypoglycemic drug.

DIARRHEA

SOMETHING IS AMISS in the digestive tract if bowel movements are soft, unformed, and liquid or more frequent than three times a day.

More often than not, diarrhea is caused by mild bouts of food-borne illness, or food poisoning. Many viruses often cause mild diarrhea as well.

Other causes of diarrhea include eating too much of a particular food, such as fresh fruit; eating foods to which one is allergic or intolerant, such as milk products; or having intestinal disorders such as colitis or irritable bowel syndrome.

If the large intestine, or colon, allows food residue to pass through quickly, moisture and nutrients do not get absorbed.

Sometimes the colon will even draw water from the body to help it hastily get rid of unwanted feces. Either can leave you dehydrated and lacking important minerals.

GARDEN HEALERS The roots of Oregon grape and goldenseal contain berberine, an antimicrobial that may be effective against harmful food-borne bacteria, and other alkaloids. They also appear to decrease colon secretion, helping decrease diarrhea. Their immune-stimulating action will help many people who have viral diarrhea as well. These herbs are often used to treat even serious cases of diarrhea when supervised by a knowledgeable health care provider. They can be taken as tea or tincture. Blackberry roots are another good diarrhea remedy.

Bilberry also has mild antimicrobial properties, plus it is an astringent and helps to tone the muscles of the colon. Eat the berries or syrup made from them or drink an infusion from the leaves. Fresh bilberries or their close cousins, blueberries, may worsen diarrhea, but dried berries are an excellent remedy for it.

All geranium and red raspberry leaves have astringent qualities, which are useful for treating diarrhea because they help the colon contract and slow down the passage of feces, giving the body a chance to withdraw water from the mass as it passes through. These herbs also bind toxins.

Mullein may be useful for reducing inflammation of the digestive tract. Other herbs such as chamomile, fennel, and peppermint may also soothe the lining of the colon.

Nettle soothes an inflamed colon but also has mild laxative properties. Be sure to use it with discretion.

In large quantities, psyllium seeds and husks, familiar as a constipation remedy, can also help diarrhea. They provide bulk to slow down the passage of liquid material through the large intestine. Use a teaspoon or less at frequent intervals. Do not take them with prunes, figs, or dates.

As soon as diarrhea has subsided enough for you to tolerate solid food, get plenty of foods rich in potassium and sodium—two major electrolytes. Garden produce, especially asparagus, beet greens, berries, citrus fruits, cruciferous vegetables, melons, plums, potatoes, salad greens, sweet potatoes, and squash, are teeming with potassium. Potato skins are especially beneficial.

Echinacea or other immune-stimulating herbs are critical during bouts of diarrhea caused by infectious microbes.

⅄ Diarrhea is a symptom—the body is trying to get rid of something harmful. It is generally recommended to let diarrhea run its course, being careful to replace fluids and electrolytes by drinking broth and eating potassium-rich vegetables. Children and

---

DIARRHEA RECIPE

2 teaspoons Oregon grape root

1 teaspoon dried leaves of bilberry OR scented geranium OR red raspberry

1–2 cloves garlic

½ teaspoon chamomile

2 cups water

Simmer Oregon grape root for 10 minutes. Remove from heat and add remaining herbs. Steep for 15 minutes. Drink warm; avoid cold liquids during bouts of diarrhea.

---

babies should be watched carefully and medical attention sought if diarrhea is severe, persists longer than one day, or worsens after one day. The same is true for adults.

⅄ If stools are bloody, get medical attention immediately.

DIGESTIVE PROBLEMS

DIGESTIVE PROBLEMS can be helped enormously by nature's pharmacy. There are plants to stimulate digestion or relax it, to help expel gas, and to soothe inflammation and pain. Most culinary herbs were used because of their ability to facilitate digestion.

GARDEN HEALERS Although people shy away from bitter foods, bitters perform a valuable function. Bitter greens, for instance, typically stimulate digestion. This means they prompt the body into making more digestive juices such as hydrochloric acid in the stomach and digestive enzymes in the intestine. Bitter foods also stimulate the gallbladder to contract and release bile, which helps break fatty foods into small enough particles that enzymes can easily finish breaking them apart for absorption. This is important because fats carry essential fatty acids, such as heart-healthy omega-3s, along with fat-soluble vitamins A, D, E, and K and carotenoids such as beta-carotene. Bitter herbs can also stimulate the appetite.

Bitter digestive stimulants include angelica, black cohosh, dandelion, skullcap, and yarrow. One cup of tea per day of one or several of these herbs should enhance digestion sufficiently; use much smaller quantities of wormwood. Dandelion is perhaps the most popular digestive aid in this lineup. Its bitter substance has been identified as taraxacin. Juniper is not considered a bitter herb, but it increases hydrochloric acid secretion in the stomach.

Carminatives dispel gas in the intestines. Herbs that lend a hand in this category include fennel, lavender, mint, rosemary, and juniper. Rosemary does double duty—it also increases digestive juices and bile like its bitter cousins. Include rosemary and fennel in your cooking to add flavor to meals. These two herbs may be especially helpful for digesting fat—include them in high-fat dishes. Make infusions of any of these herbs, and drink when you have trouble with excessive gas and need to soothe an upset stomach. Fennel is even mild enough for children and is especially helpful to them when combined with chamomile.

Antispasmodic herbs are those that relax muscle spasms. Herbs with this property put an end to stomach and intestinal cramps. A cup of tea of one or more of these will do the trick: black cohosh, chamomile, lavender, lemon balm, mint, skullcap, valerian, wild yam, wormwood, and yarrow. See individual profiles for recommended dosages.

Other helpful herbs include those with demulcent properties. This means they soothe, coat, and lubricate. Marshmallow, mullein, and oats are good demulcents. Several cups of marshmallow or mullein tea can be enjoyed per day. Oats can be used in their traditional form as oatmeal.

Ginger, a tropical herb not easily grown in the average garden, is also a good digestive aid and is number one when it comes to thwarting nausea. Numerous clinical trials support this use of ginger. European angelica is also a digestive stimulant similar to ginger.

⅄ If you have excessive stomach acid, do not use digestive stimulants, including bitters and ginger. Wormwood should be used internally only in small amounts and generally only when you are under the care of a health care professional trained in its use.

EAR INFECTION

AN EARACHE usually indicates an allergy or an ear infection. Earaches often accompany a cold or sore throat because it's so easy for undesirable microbes to make their way from the nose and throat up the Eustachian tube and into the inner and middle ear.

Children are especially susceptible because their Eustachian tube is very short and mostly horizontal, making it easy for mucus to pass from the back of the throat directly into the middle ear.

GARDEN HEALERS If you or your child succumb to infections easily, use herbal eardrops at the first sign of a cold. Mullein is the herb of choice for this condition because it is so effective. Infuse mullein's essential essences into olive oil and use as eardrops. If desired, add garlic to take advantage of its antimicrobial properties. See the recipe on this page.

EARACHE REMEDY

1 cup mullein flowers; fresh is best but use dried if you can't obtain fresh

1 cup olive oil, or enough to cover flowers

4 cloves garlic, chopped or crushed (optional)

Place mullein flowers in a small saucepan. Add olive oil until flowers are covered. Heat on low for several hours, just until fragrant. If using garlic, add it during the last hour. Cool and strain. When ready to use, shake well. With an ear dropper, administer 2–10 drops into the outer ear canal, three times per day or at bedtime if the earache is less severe. Keep the head tilted for a few minutes to allow the oil to penetrate the ear, and hold in place with a piece of cotton. Store in a tightly sealed jar in a cool, dark place.

Combine goldenseal, purple coneflower, mint, and chamomile into a sipping tea to help reduce the risk of ear infection during a cold or sore throat. The goldenseal (or Oregon grape root) along with purple coneflower will boost immune function so infectious bacteria can be conquered, hopefully before they cause trouble. Mint contains menthol, which has strong antiseptic properties, killing bacteria and viruses. In hot tea, the menthol-infused steam makes its way into nasal and throat passages, as well as into the Eustachian tube. Chamomile reduces inflammation, allowing fluid drainage from the Eustachian tube and preventing buildup of mucus and bacteria.

A wholesome diet rich in natural, unprocessed foods will provide necessary nourishment to prevent ear infections. Garden produce can provide many of the needed nutrients, such as vitamins A and C, that enhance the activity of white blood cells. Vitamin A, as beta-carotene in fruits and vegetables, maintains the integrity of skin and mucous membrane cells. Healthy cells are more resistant to disease. Adequate amounts of protein are needed, too, to make antibodies—the body's warriors against foreign substances such as bacteria and viruses. Garden fresh beans provide protein and fiber. Fresh foods rich in flavonoids also boost immune function. These include red- and purple-colored produce such as apples, purple cabbage, and berries. Limit simple sugars; in excess they depress immune function.

Witch hazel is helpful in treating swimmer's ear. Make a tincture of witch hazel, goldenseal, or Oregon grape root and calendula. Apply to the outer ear. Rue can also diminish the pain and inflammation.

Ⴟ Ear infections are serious business. Prompt medical attention ensures that the inner ear does not sustain damage. Ear infections sometimes require antibiotics.

FEVER

A FEVER IS one of the body's natural healing processes. By heating up, your body can stimulate the immune system to destroy infectious bacteria and viruses.

Although it can be uncomfortable, a fever should be allowed to do its job in most cases. Suppressing a fever may prolong it, since the body must use other means to overcome the "bug."

GARDEN HEALERS Several herbs have diaphoretic, or sweat-inducing, properties. By initiating or increasing perspiration, these herbs rid the body of the toxins contributing to the illness and help keep the fever from going too high. Thus, the healing is accomplished and the fever breaks.

Such common garden herbs as angelica, elderberry, rosemary, and yarrow are all diaphoretic.

Drinking infusions of these will help the fever process. However, continued sweating can cause dangerous dehydration if you don't consume adequate fluids.

Of course, it's important to support immune function during a fever. Use immune boosters such as echinacea, licorice, chamomile, goldenseal, or Oregon grape and foods rich in vitamin C and flavonoids.

⅄ If a fever lasts more than three days or is above 102°F in adults—or for any fever in infants and children—seek medical attention promptly.

GALLSTONES

GALLSTONES OCCUR when one of the compounds in bile, particularly cholesterol, becomes so saturated that it forms a solid. If a gallstone lodges in the bile duct, it can cause severe pain, inflammation, infection, and sometimes even jaundice due to the backup of bile.

GARDEN HEALERS Preventing gallstones is preferable to treating them after they have formed. Research indicates that a high-fiber, low-fat, low-cholesterol diet rich in vitamins C and E helps prevent stones from forming. This is just what your healing garden offers you. Vegetables and fruits tend to be high in fiber and vitamins, low in fat, and cholesterol free.

In addition, some herbs stimulate the gallbladder, promoting the flow of bile. Dandelion and milk thistle are particularly useful. They contain bitter substances—taraxacin in dandelion and silymarin in milk thistle—that stimulate bile production. Increasing the amount of bile produced decreases its concentration. And the greater volume is also more likely to flush out a stone. These herbs can be taken as tea or tincture or eaten steamed. Trim the sharp edges off young milk thistle leaves. Mix them with dandelion greens and steam as you would spinach; you can even eat them raw.

Oregon grape enhances blood flow to the liver and increases bile production. It can be combined with dandelion and milk thistle in a tea. This blend is even more effective when mixed with herbs such as chamomile, marshmallow, and slippery elm, which have relaxing and soothing properties. This mixture will also help decrease gallbladder inflammation.

Rosemary stimulates bile production, too, while also eliminating any spasms that might occur in the bile duct. It is well-known for aiding fat digestion and is often used as an herb in high-fat dishes. Its flavor helps to cut the richness of fat.

Several studies have shown concentrated mint oil capsules can, if taken for several months,

ANTI-GALLSTONE TEA

1 teaspoon Oregon grape root

2 teaspoons marshmallow root

2 teaspoons dandelion leaves, dried (or 1 teaspoon root)

1 teaspoon peppermint

4 cups water

Simmer roots in water for 15 minutes. Remove from heat and add dandelion leaves. Let steep 15 minutes. Strain. Drink immediately or refrigerate. Use as a tea throughout the day, preferably after meals.

help break down small gallstones.

Wild yam is another herb that increases bile flow and is also said to lessen the pain of gallstones. Like rosemary, it is an antispasmodic herb.

⅄ Ultrasound is needed to definitively diagnose gallstones. A qualified health care practitioner should monitor herbal treatment of them. Once stones have formed, they can cause urgent medical problems if they block the bile duct. In that case, surgery may be necessary.

HAY FEVER

HAY FEVER IS AN allergic reaction to pollen characterized by sneezing; inflamed, watery, itchy eyes; and thin nasal discharge.

GARDEN HEALERS Vitamin C is a natural antihistamine, helping to reduce nasal secretions and inflammation. Flavonoids such as quercetin, rutin, and hesperidin also have antihistamine properties and work well with vitamin C. Luckily, this vitamin and the flavonoids occur together in many favorite garden foods, such as berries, plums, citrus fruits, peppers, spinach, and broccoli.

Nettle is useful for reducing hay fever symptoms. Take a tincture made from the leaves. Use 2–4 mL three times per day. Nettle leaves can also be taken in tea or capsule form.

Angelica comes to the rescue for hay fever as well as other allergic reactions. It contains compounds that block the body's production of certain antibodies (IgE) that are made as the result of an allergic response. Use about ½ teaspoon per cup of water for tea.

Many studies have proved licorice's ability to reduce allergic symptoms and decrease inflammation. Substances in this herb are able to enhance the body's cortisol, a hormone that decreases inflammation. Licorice makes your body's own cortisol last longer, reducing inflammation without ill side effects.

Chili pepper, or cayenne, contains capsaicin. This active ingredient helps desensitize the mucosa that line the airways, thus preventing them from secreting excessive fluids and becoming inflamed when exposed to irritants.

⅄ In larger doses taken for long periods, licorice can deplete the body of potassium unless it is deglycyrrhizinated. In susceptible people taking large doses, licorice can raise blood pressure.

Headaches

HEADACHES CAN BE classified into two main categories: general tension headaches and migraine headaches.

Tension headaches are bilateral, relatively mild attacks of head pain. Migraines are usually accompanied by changes in vision, sensitivity to light, and sometimes nausea. They are thought to be related to abnormal dilation and constriction of blood vessels in the brain. A variety of factors can trigger either type of headache, including hormonal changes, stress, and allergies to food and sunlight.

GARDEN HEALERS Feverfew is notorious for its ability to prevent and stop headaches. If one or two leaves are taken on a daily basis, it reduces the frequency of migraines, and if one does occur, it tends to be less severe than normal. Feverfew may work in several ways: It limits the secretion of compounds that cause inflammation, it prevents blood vessels from constricting, and it prevents the neurotransmitter serotonin from being released from certain cells. Feverfew accomplishes all this with minimal side effects.

One of the active ingredients in feverfew is called parthenolide. Research indicates that taking 250 µg of this substance per day as part of an extract of the whole leaf on a continuous basis is the minimum dose needed to reduce the number of migraines you have, as well as their severity. It usually takes four to six weeks before effects are noticed. Feverfew is best taken in capsule form or as a fresh leaf.

Ginkgo biloba may also be of assistance if you have migraines. It improves circulation, decreases inflammation, and inhibits the production of a substance called platelet-activating factor that may be linked to migraines.

If you have frequent headaches, it is important to identify what might be causing them. Keeping

HOMEMADE HEADACHE PILLS

2 tablespoons valerian, dried	2 tablespoons chamomile, dried
2 tablespoons skullcap, dried	2 tablespoons peppermint, dried
2 tablespoons rosemary, dried	Honey

Grind all herbs in a coffee grinder or food processor until powdered. (These will break down rapidly and should be used within two weeks of grinding.) Blend with enough honey to bind. Break off small, pill-sized pieces. Roll into a ball, then flatten slightly. Dry. Store in tightly sealed container. Use 1 or 2 to help relieve a tension headache.

a diary of foods and reactions may help. Food allergies and sensitivities often trigger an attack; eliminating them may eliminate most painful headaches.

The pain of tension headaches can be diminished with herbs that have sedative and antispasmodic properties. The sedative herbs will relax you, decrease anxiety, and help you feel calmer. The antispasmodic herbs will relax muscles in the head and neck and can also help relax muscles that line the arteries, preventing them from constricting and reducing blood flow to the brain.

To get both sedative and antispasmodic effects, use valerian, skullcap, lemon balm, and passion flower. Make a tea or tincture of these herbs at the first sign of a headache and drink a cup or two. You can also include herbs such as lavender and mullein. On the other hand, if you're looking more for muscle relaxation, add chamomile, rosemary, or mint.

✗ Do not use feverfew if you are pregnant or nursing. Eating raw feverfew leaves may occasionally cause mouth sores; you may prefer to dry them and put them in capsules. The side effects of this herb are usually mild—occasional gastrointestinal upset or nervousness.

MENOPAUSE

MENOPAUSE USUALLY occurs between the ages

of 45 and 55. At this time, menstrual cycles cease, and there is a drop in hormone levels, especially those of estrogen and progesterone.

Menopause is accompanied by myriad symptoms ranging from moodiness and insomnia to hot flashes and vaginal dryness. In the Western world, the decrease in hormones increases the risk of osteoporosis and heart disease. The role of diet and exercise and other environmental factors is also important.

GARDEN HEALERS Some plants and herbs contain compounds called phytoestrogens that mimic a woman's own estrogen in a mild way, helping to prevent some of the symptoms and risks associated with menopause. Soybean products such as tofu, tempeh, and roasted soy nuts are rich in phytoestrogens. Women in Asian cultures who consume large amounts of soy foods do not experience hot flashes, nor does their rate of osteoporosis and heart disease

rise dramatically with menopause, as it does in the United States Although you probably can't grow enough soybeans to make tofu, there are other plants and herbs that can be useful.

Licorice has estrogenic effects and is successfully used to treat menopausal symptoms. Black cohosh, alfalfa, and red clover contain phytoestrogens, too. Hot flashes may diminish with the regular use of one or more of these herbs. Eighty milligrams per day of black cohosh extract, taken in divided doses, is beneficial to some women. Oregon grape and dandelion root are two other herbs that some claim help to reduce hot flashes, but this has not yet been confirmed.

It was thought for some time that wild yam contained a substance similar to progesterone, a female hormone. Unfortunately, the compound it does contain cannot be converted into the needed hormone in the body. However, in the laboratory a progesteronelike substance can be made from wild yam and may be useful for retaining bone density and relieving symptoms. Other wild yam compounds and their actions may be of benefit to menopausal women.

Lignans, which are a component of fiber, also act as phytoestrogens. Lignans are found in flax, whole grains, legumes, and some vegetables.

The vegetables in your garden can also contribute loads of vitamin C and bioflavonoids, both of which may help relieve hot flashes. Although most vegetables contain some vitamin C, those with large amounts include broccoli, beet greens, peppers, parsley, salad greens, citrus fruits, melons, berries, and apricots. Bioflavonoids are also usually found in foods high in vitamin C. For instance, the white membrane on the outside of a peeled orange and the whitish ribs inside a bell pepper are extremely rich in bioflavonoids. Be sure to eat them rather than throw them

away. Berries, including some not normally cultivated in a garden, contain helpful flavonoids. Hawthorn berries, elderberries, and bilberries are all rich in this substance.

Vitamins A and E, aloe vera, and calendula are recommended to counteract vaginal dryness. A solution of calendula can be used as a douche.

Chinese angelica, or dong quai, helps to balance postmenopausal hormones. It, too, reduces hot flash symptoms. Use tea, extract, tincture, or capsules. A common dose is 3–4 g per day.

If insomnia is one of your symptoms, try drinking a soothing cup of chamomile and valerian tea an hour or so before bedtime.

Some women find that gamma-linolenic acid, an essential fatty acid derived from evening primrose, borage, or currant seed oil, helps ease them through menopause.

⅄ Licorice can elevate blood pressure unless it is deglycyrrhizinated. Do not use Chinese angelica if you are pregnant or nursing or during menstruation.

MENSTRUATION

MENSTRUAL CRAMPS, heavy or light periods, and pre-menstrual syndrome (PMS) can make a woman uncomfortable at "that time of the month."

PMS includes a cluster of about 150 symptoms. The most frequently reported problems include fluid retention and bloating, breast tenderness, irritability and depression, skin blemishes, fatigue, and carbohydrate cravings.

GARDEN HEALERS Diuretic herbs can help take care of fluid retention and the feeling of bloat that often accompanies menstruation. Parsley, dandelion, hydrangea, angelica, and horsetail all have diuretic properties. Drink infusions or decoctions of these herbs.

Breast tenderness, skin blemishes, and cravings are typically caused by hormone imbalances. Chinese angelica, or dong quai, helps to stabilize hormone levels. One method is to mark on the calendar the time in your cycle that you experience these symptoms. Start taking tea or tincture of dong quai several days before the anticipated problem time. Stop taking dong quai as soon as your period starts.

For a PMS headache, try some of the suggestions in the "Headache" profile, pages 230–231.

Painful menstrual cramps are a frequent complaint; antispasmodics are invaluable for repressing them. Herbs that have a particularly good reputation for easing menstrual cramps include black cohosh, valerian, wild yam, yarrow, chamomile, and feverfew. Make decoctions or infusions of these and start drinking them a day or two before you expect cramps to start; take every two hours during the most acute phase.

Red raspberry leaves tone the uterus and also help prevent

menstrual cramps. This herb needs to be taken consistently over a long period of time to get this benefit. If menstrual flow is heavy, red raspberry leaves will help control it. Yarrow is also instrumental in reducing excessive menstrual flow. Use tea or tinctures several times per day.

If you have the opposite problem, very light periods, and you need to increase menstrual flow, angelica can coax the situation. This herb will also help regulate the menses.

The underlying cause of heavy or light periods should be determined before using herbs. Consult a holistic practitioner.

Several herbs contain oils that have proved very beneficial in reducing PMS symptoms. The herbs can be grown in your garden, but it takes commercial preparation to get enough strong oil from them. Evening primrose, black currant, and borage contain gamma-linolenic acid (GLA). Three thousand milligrams of evening primrose oil per day, taken in divided doses, alleviates many PMS symptoms for some women. Begin taking this ten days before menses are expected to start. Traditionally, evening primrose is eaten as a food and may be helpful if eaten frequently.

ORAL CARE

INFLAMED OR bleeding gums, gingivitis, thrush, bad breath, toothaches, and teething are some of the conditions that plague the mouth. A variety of herbs in your garden will improve, soothe, or eliminate these problems.

GARDEN HEALERS Calendula and echinacea soothe sore gums and reduce inflammation. They are an excellent treatment for *Candida albicans*, an opportunistic yeast that causes thrush in the mouth. Dab affected areas with calendula tincture diluted with an equal amount of water. For gums, make a strong infusion and swish it in the mouth for several minutes. You can either spit it out or swallow it.

HERBAL MOUTHWASH

1 teaspoon rosemary, dried
1 teaspoon mint, dried
1 teaspoon fennel seed
2½ cups water

Boil water and pour over herbs. Let steep 15–20 minutes. Strain and refrigerate. Use as a gargle. Rosemary is a good antiseptic. Mint provides a sweet smell to the breath.

A couple of drops of lavender oil is also good at clearing up *Candida albicans*, as well as reducing inflammation and healing sores. Infected gums are successfully treated with goldenseal or Oregon grape, too. Their berberine content gives them antimicrobial effects, killing off offending bacteria. Rosemary helps heal canker sores and has antiseptic properties.

Parsley is a natural breath sweetener. Instead of sending it back to the kitchen on your plate, nibble this herb after your meal. Not only will you have better breath, but you'll also get a boost of vitamins A and C and the minerals calcium and iron. Licorice sweetens breath, too,

and is frequently used to flavor and sweeten herbal toothpaste and mouthwashes. Fennel has a similar action and will also help if you have gas.

Oil of cloves, a tropical spice you can't grow in your garden, is good to have on hand for toothaches or teething. Rub a little on the gums.

SORE THROAT

A SORE THROAT can accompany a cold or flu, or it can be the result of overuse of the voice or irritants such as cigarette smoke.

GARDEN HEALERS Herbs can reduce pain and inflammation, provide temporary relief, and help heal raw throat tissues. Typical immune boosters such as echinacea and goldenseal or Oregon grape root are good to take when you have a sore throat that is caused by a cold or flu. Garlic will fight off offending bacteria or viruses. Try adding it raw to your salad and other dishes.

Mucilaginous herbs can ease any sore throat. Marshmallow and slippery elm do a great job. Gargling with astringent herbs will alleviate discomfort. Raspberry or blackberry leaves along with elder flowers are good for this purpose. Combine them with marshmallow and licorice for a soothing effect. Cayenne pepper, believe it or not, helps to stop pain, so add it to your gargling mixture. It is crucial to gargle all these herbs before swallowing them.

SPLINTERS

SLIVERS OF WOOD, metal, or glass that become embedded in the skin need to be removed to avoid infection. Use sterilized tweezers or a sewing needle to ease the splinter out, then wash the wound with herbs that have antiseptic and anti-inflammatory properties.

GARDEN HEALERS Herbs that have both antiseptic and anti-inflammatory properties include St. John's wort, chamomile, elderberry, goldenseal, Oregon grape, licorice, wormwood, and yarrow. A strong infusion of one or more of these herbs can be used to wash the area where a splinter has poked through the skin.

Although the huge and now uncommon slippery elm tree is not likely to be in your garden, its bark is very useful when it

---

HERBAL THROAT LOZENGES

3 tablespoons licorice, powdered

3 tablespoons marshmallow or slippery elm, powdered

3 tablespoons red raspberry leaves, powdered

1 teaspoon cayenne pepper

10 drops scented geranium, sage, or rosemary essential oil

Honey

Cornstarch

Mix herbal powders together with just enough honey to make a thick goo. Add essential oil and mix well with fork or fingers. Pinch off small pieces, roll into balls, and flatten slightly to form a lozenge. Toss lightly in a bowl with a little cornstarch. Set to dry for 12 hours. Store in an airtight container.

---

comes to splinters. A poultice made with the powder of slippery elm will coax the splinter out of the skin, helping you remove it quickly and with little poking around. It also helps heal the damaged tissue. You can substitute marshmallow root for slippery elm.

SPRAINS, BRUISES, AND SORE MUSCLES

SPRAINS RESULT from overstretching ligaments that surround joints. Bruises are the result of external pressure that's hard enough to break blood vessels. Sore muscles result from unusual movement or overexertion. Luckily, nature provides remedies to heal these conditions and help you feel better sooner.

GARDEN HEALERS Bruises caused from light pressure indicate delicate blood vessels that could use some strengthening. Eat produce from your garden that is rich in vitamin C and flavonoids—both of which contribute to the integrity and elasticity of blood vessels. Such foods include berries of all types, including elderberry, hawthorn, and bilberry. Plums, citrus fruits, bell peppers, and broccoli are also rich in these nutrients. Herbs that are chock-full of flavonoids include butcher's broom, nettle, Oregon grape, rosemary, and skullcap; try some of these in tea. Infusions of witch hazel, wormwood, and chamomile can also be applied externally to speed the healing of bruises.

Applying a compress of St. John's wort, witch hazel, wintergreen, wormwood, or chamomile can help a sprain heal quickly.

Arnica is one of the best pain relievers for sore muscles as well as sprains. Make a salve or liniment from this comforting plant. Several herbs, including valerian, skullcap, and rosemary, help decrease muscle spasms; drink tea made from them. Black cohosh, chamomile, and mint applied topically decrease pain and inflammation. Lavender oil makes a fragrant and relaxing massage oil for sore or stressed muscles. Cayenne pepper, a warming herb, will increase circulation when used in a liniment. Increasing circulation helps in the removal of substances such as lactic acid that are produced by overworked muscles.

SWOLLEN VEINS

VARICOSE VEINS and hemorrhoids are examples of swollen veins. Unlike arteries, which carry blood away from the heart, veins carry blood to the heart, often against the force of gravity.

Small valves in some veins assist in the process. Any pressure on the legs will strain the veins in the lower extremities and the valves within them.

Conditions that cause leg pressure include obesity, pregnancy, heavy lifting, and lengthy standing or sitting. Blood pools, veins swell, and thus the familiar blue varicose veins are born. Although the veins in the rectal area don't have valves, they can still swell from these causes, forming hemorrhoids. Straining during bowel movements, a common practice when you're constipated, and pregnancy both increase pressure on the rectal veins.

GARDEN HEALERS Butcher's broom, St. John's wort, and witch hazel are particularly helpful in relieving the ache and discomfort of varicose veins and hemorrhoids.

Butcher's broom contains compounds called ruscogenins. These substances decrease inflammation while constricting the vein. Taken internally, 100 mg ruscogenins—usually a whole herb extract—taken three times per day is beneficial. German researchers verify that this herb helps to tighten, strengthen, and decrease inflammation in veins, helping blood flow up the legs. A compress of butcher's broom may be applied externally.

St. John's wort also reduces inflammation and is used externally and internally for both ailments. Use it externally in salves, oils, or tinctures, rubbing them into the affected area. Drink infusions of St. John's wort to provide nutrients and compounds that will nourish the stressed veins. This herb should be used fresh or freeze-dried, as it loses its medicinal properties if air-dried.

Witch hazel, the famous astringent herb, is full of tannins, gallic acids, and essential oils. While you can take it internally as tea, it is best to make a strong decoction for use as a compress. When applied to hemorrhoids, witch hazel reduces pain and swelling. It also tightens and soothes aching varicose veins and reduces inflammation.

When applied externally, lavender, too, will reduce inflammation and help heal these enlarged vessels. Yarrow, horse chestnut, calendula tincture, and chamomile are also helpful used topically.

Flavonoid-rich foods help reduce the risk of developing varicose veins and hemorrhoids because of their strengthening action on the veins. These compounds reduce fragility and tone the muscles that line the walls of the vessels. Blue, red, and purple foods, such as berries, cherries, and plums, are rich in flavonoids, as are some herbs such as St. John's wort, hawthorn, linden flowers, and bilberry.

Rosemary not only strengthens and protects vessels with its antioxidants, but also improves circulation, thus helping to alleviate both varicose veins and hemorrhoids. Use liberally in foods, and make a liniment to apply topically.

ULCERS

GASTRIC ULCERS are those that occur in the stomach, while duodenal ulcers are located in the upper portion of the small intestine; the term peptic ulcer commonly encompasses both types.

H. pylori bacteria cause many peptic ulcers. This organism or other irritants can break down the mucosal lining of the stomach, allowing digestive acid to eat away at the underlying tissue. If you over-produce acid, as can happen in times of stress, this worsens the condition. However, many people with gastric ulcers in particular actually make too little acid.

GARDEN HEALERS Long thought to aggravate ulcers, cayenne pepper in moderation actually helps heal them in some cases. Stimulating blood flow to bring healing nutrients to the area, this member of the nightshade family can be good therapy for ulcers. Taking ¼ teaspoon in 1 cup of hot water per day is all it takes.

Cabbage and its juice are also known for their ulcer-healing abilities. Researchers have found that ulcer patients who drink 1 quart of raw cabbage juice a day often heal their ulcers in five days. Those who eat cabbage also have quicker healing times,

although not as dramatic as with the juice.

Garden produce rich in flavonoids may be helpful, too. Studies indicate that some bioflavonoids inhibit the growth of *H. pylori*. These compounds are also useful as anti-inflammatories. Eat red- and purple-colored foods, such as plums, berries, and red cabbage. Parsley and onions are also good sources. Garlic and licorice have also been shown to kill *H. Pylori* in test tubes.

Bilberry is used frequently in Russia to treat ulcers. It reduces inflammation in the stomach and intestines and protects their fragile mucous membranes. Calendula is also good for ulcers due to its wound-healing ability. It is slightly unpleasant to drink as tea; add calendula tincture to a pleasantly flavored beverage.

Chamomile works in a different way. It decreases inflammation, thus speeding up the healing process. Apigenin, a flavonoid contained in chamomile, helps to combat *H. pylori* bacteria.

Several strong cups of tea per day may be helpful.

Licorice mimics the action of chamomile, but is even more effective. It soothes inflammation and encourages the stomach to protect itself from acid. This herb helps improve and maintain the integrity of stomach and small intestine linings by stimulating the production of a substance called mucin. When the lining of the stomach and duodenum, the upper portion of the small intestine, are well coated with mucin, ulcers are less likely to start. Use deglycyrrhizinated licorice (DGL) to avoid raising blood pressure. Take chewable tablets shortly before meals and several hours before bedtime. Typically 250–500 mg are recommended.

Marshmallow is also a soothing agent. Its mucilage calms inflammation and helps heal ulcers. Slippery elm, with its mucilaginous gel, also soothes the lining of the stomach and small intestine. (It's best to stir powder into water that's at room temperature.) Peppermint is another good herb for reducing the inflammation associated with peptic ulcers. Its main active ingredient, menthol, is antibacterial, so it may help get rid of *H. pylori*. In some cases it stimulates digestion and may increase acidity, so use with care if this happens.

Yarrow has been clinically seen to make blood clot faster and stop bleeding. If you have bleeding ulcers, yarrow tea or tincture may help control the unwanted bleeding. Yarrow is also excellent at reducing inflammation.

✗ Ulcers, especially those that bleed (sometimes noted as black stools), need medical attention. Discuss the combination of conventional and herbal treatment with a physician. Do not use chamomile if you are allergic to ragweed, aster, or chrysanthemum.

URINARY TRACT INFECTION

OFTEN CALLED a bladder infection, a urinary tract

infection (UTI) can affect not only the bladder but also the kidney and the urethra, the tube that carries urine out of the body.

Painful and inconvenient, a UTI results in frequent urges to urinate with little production of urine and is accompanied by a severe burning sensation. Women are most often affected, and the infections sometimes recur frequently.

GARDEN HEALERS There are several herbs that help tackle a UTI. Goldenseal and Oregon grape both contain berberine and other alkaloids that kill bacteria and stimulate the immune system. These herbs also appear to inhibit infection-causing bacteria from adhering to the wall of the bladder, so they are sloughed off in urine.

Though not a garden plant, cranberry is an essential remedy for preventing and treating UTIs. Drink 16–24 ounces per day of unsweetened juice or use capsules.

Another herb, uva ursi, helps to kill bacteria. It possesses a compound called arbutin, which the body converts into a bacteria-killing substance. In Europe, uva ursi is widely used to treat UTIs. Alkaline urine is necessary for arbutin to be most effective. Drinking large (more than 16 ounces) amounts of cranberry juice can affect the pH of urine and interfere with arbutin. Sometimes it is necessary to take bicarbonate of soda to make the urine alkaline enough for arbutin to work.

Herbs that have diuretic abilities, increasing the amount of urine that passes through the bladder, help wash away bacteria. Hydrangea, parsley, and dandelion leaves are diuretics. Parsley's seeds also contain a substance that is sometimes used to treat UTIs; it also helps reduce inflammation. Horsetail is an astringent diuretic encouraging urine flow and halting bleeding from the urinary tract.

Marshmallow soothes inflamed areas and enhances immune

function to help fight off unwanted bacteria. Mullein also is known for reducing urinary tract inflammation.

The leaves, flowers, and especially the seeds of nasturtium contain natural antibiotics that may be helpful in preventing UTIs. Horseradish root also contains an antibiotic substance along with a good dose of vitamin C, both of which may be helpful in treating this condition.

Vitamins A and C, richly found in the produce from your healing garden, are good for preventing UTIs. The vitamin A, usually in the form of beta-carotene in plants, helps cells form properly and maintains their integrity, making them more resistant to invasion from unfriendly bacteria. Vitamin C not only helps the immune system with production of certain infection-fighters, but in large amounts it can increase urine's acidity. The bacteria that cause this infection do not survive well under acidic conditions, so vitamin C tends to inhibit them. However, it takes more vitamin C than can be obtained from foods. At least 5,000 mg of this nutrient are needed to significantly acidify the urine; one orange contains about 60 mg.

- Unless you are quickly successful with herbal remedies, it's very important to seek medical care promptly. During and after a UTI, always follow up with a health care provider. Symptoms may disappear, but the infectious bacteria can make its way up to the kidney and cause damage and even death. Only a urinalysis can reveal whether all offending bacteria are out of the entire urinary tract. Always seek medical advice if there is blood in the urine.
- Do not use goldenseal, Oregon grape, or uva ursi if you are pregnant or nursing.

WARTS

CAUSED BY A VIRUS, mildly contagious, and usually unsightly, warts indicate a

sluggish immune system. Combating warts is a two-step process: adopting behaviors that support immunity and using plants from your garden to destroy the wart itself.

GARDEN HEALERS First of all, boost immune function. Base your diet on whole grains and fresh garden produce, eat only small amounts of simple sugars, and get plenty of rest. The body makes certain immune factors only when you're sleeping.

The main immune-boosting herb that has been clinically studied is echinacea. Others include licorice, goldenseal, and elderberry; all can be taken internally. Echinacea is quite safe to use for extended periods in certain severe immune problems, although some falsely advise to only use it for short periods.

The allium family helps do away with the actual wart. Crush a clove of garlic and tape a small amount of it to the growth. Protect surrounding skin to avoid blistering. Alternatively, cut an onion in half, hollow out one side, and fill with salt. As the salt draws the juice out of the onion, use the liquid to paint the wart several times a day.

A chunk of aspirin taped to the wart will produce the same effect. Herbs rich in salicylic acid, the active ingredient in aspirin, may be helpful, too. Mash fresh yarrow and apply it to the wart.

Another herb that diminishes the unwanted growth is fresh dandelion. Break a dandelion stem or leaf and apply the white sap to the wart.

YEAST INFECTION

VAGINAL YEAST infections are characterized by intense itching and soreness accompanied by a thick white discharge. These uncomfortable symptoms are most often caused by a fungus called *Candida albicans*.

This organism thrives in moist, warm areas, making the vagina a perfect home for it. Normally other microorganisms keep *Candida* in check, but when this yeast grows profusely it causes a yeast infection.

GARDEN HEALERS *Candida* is a yeast that is classified as a fungus. Yeast thrives on sugars delivered by the bloodstream, so go light on your garden's fruit during an infection. Eating plenty of vegetables, though, will give you the nutrients needed to boost immunity. Echinacea also provides support for immune function during this time.

Many herbs have the ability to conquer yeast. Calendula, goldenseal, rosemary, cedar, and myrrh all have antifungal properties. Make strong decoctions or infusions of these herbs to ease itching and burning; use either internally as a douche or apply externally with pads that have been soaked in it.

Garlic has strong antifungal and antiyeast abilities. It is particularly good at inhibiting the growth of *Candida*. If you can tolerate it, chew and swallow at least 1 raw clove or more per day. This needn't be taken alone. It may be more palatable to mince or press 1 clove and sprinkle it on your daily salad or any other dish you prefer.

The friendly bacteria *Lactobacillus acidophilus* is helpful taken orally or inserted as you would a suppository in the vagina. It is available over-the-counter in capsule and powder form, or you can use yogurt containing active cultures.

⅄ Garlic is an anticoagulant, too; inform your physician if you take anticoagulants.